33 1585 8165

Presented to

Julie

From

Dr. Barbie L. Breathitt

Date

July 10, 2021

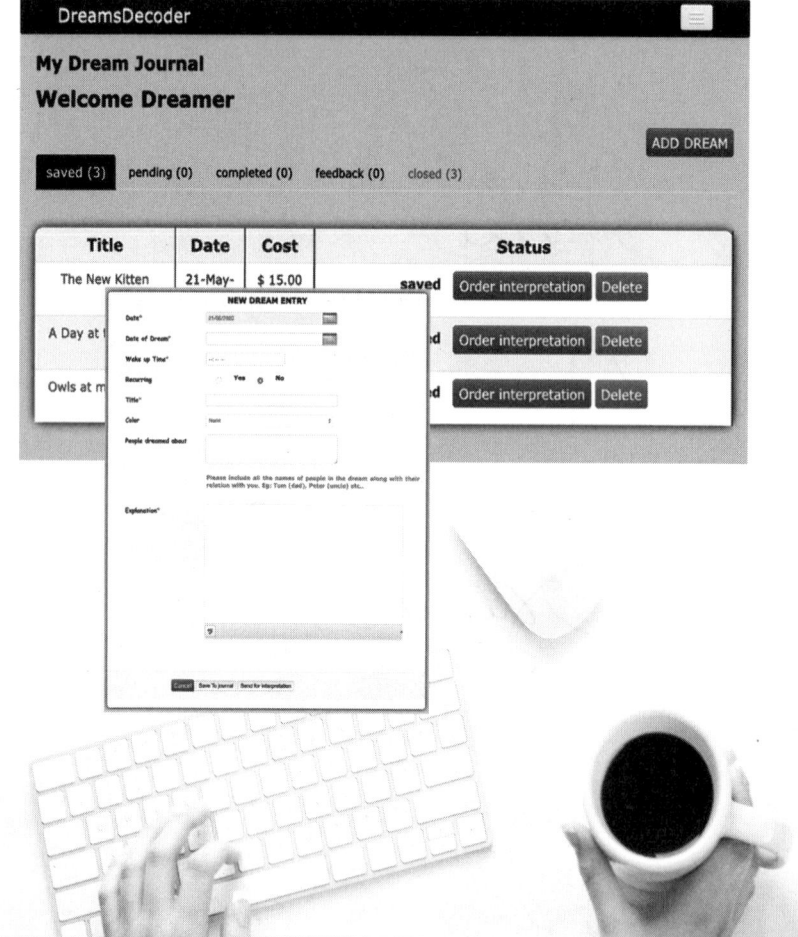

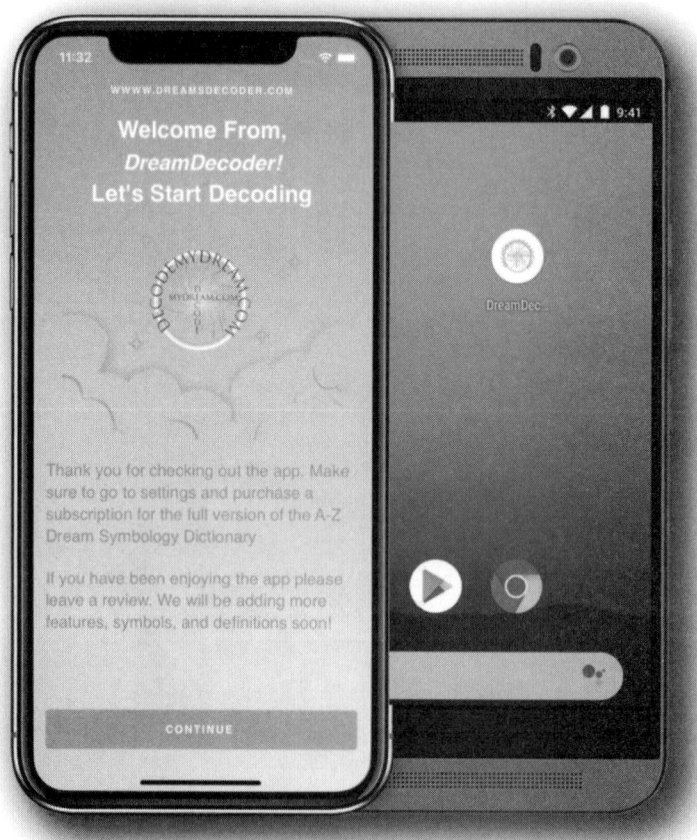

Endorsements

In my most recent book published by Charisma House, *The Passover Prophecies: How God is Realigning Hearts and Nations in Crisis,* I wrote, "We must be a people of imagination like the early pioneers of nations. Isaiah 26 is wonderfully translated in the Passion Translation Bible. I love the way verse 3 is phrased: *those whose imaginations are consumed with you* (Isa. 26:3). The Hebrew word translated "imagination" is *yester,* meaning "form, concept, framework, imagination, mind". A human imagination wholly owned by the Holy Spirit is one of the most powerful redemptive forces on earth.

These times call for a critical, God-filled imagination. This will create a new framework and conceptualization of all the problems around us. Our minds should be fixed on and become consumed by Him. This is what will unleash the supernatural creativity resident in all of the redeemed and will give birth to the exploits necessary for our triumph. In this season, we must reform our minds and imaginations. We must gather raw materials, then shape them into form and identify our future. Our concepts, frameworks, minds and imaginations must unlock into new forms and identities to meet and triumph in the era ahead.

Dr. Barbie Breathitt's five book series, *IMAGINE,* has captured the essence of God's plans to reinvent the church in the fullness of Christ's creative, life-giving, resurrection power with signs and wonders following. Each individual believer must take on his or her Christlike identity as a Son of God to move forward into this era, as One New Man arises to demonstrate God's glory on earth as it is in heaven!

Dr. Chuck D. Pierce
President, Glory of Zion International Ministries
President, Global Spheres in Corinth, Texas

God's ways are higher than our ways, and yet we are invited to co-labor with Christ as partakers in His divine nature. Pioneering ideas in her new book series *IMAGINE*, will open you up to your limitless potential. You will come to know that God created you to navigate life with the mind of Christ, and by faith, you can tap into a Spirit-inspired, creative process that is aligned with God's heart.

Dr. Breathitt's books will help you to understand your call to walk in a prophetic relationship with Jesus and to unlock the powerful truths available to all who believe in Him. This is a fresh invitation to imagine with God, to dream with Him for the future and to access and implement heaven's answers to the world's problems to advance God's Kingdom.

Dr. Ché Ahn
Founder and President, Harvest International Ministry
Founding and Senior Pastor, HROCK Church, Pasadena, CA
International Chancellor, Wagner University
Founder, Ché Ahn Ministries

Many copy or imitate others. Some create a model for others to learn from, and some are innovative. But few are innovators. Others learn a subject matter, then reach a peak and just plain plateau and cease advancing. Then there are those who become constant learners as a lifestyle, filling their heart and soul with the creative realms of God. Dr. Barbie Breathitt is cut from this type of creative fabric.

As an educator and prophetic interpreter/analyst, this consecrated woman of God consistently takes us on an exciting journey of discovery. Can you imagine that? As you partake of Barbie's teachings and her adventurous spirit carved from the boundaries of the Word of God, you, too, will grow in your prophetic imagination into a place where dreams really do come true!

Dr. James W Goll
Founder, God Encounters Ministries and GOLL Ideation LLC
Life Language Communications Coach

Dr. Barbie L. Breathitt is on the cutting edge of using her God-appointed seer gifting to help people gain an enhanced understanding of how God created and operates through the imagination, so that His people can apprehend the mysteries and purposes of God and manifest His glory in the earthly realm."

Cindy Jacobs
Generals International, Dallas, Texas

Beautiful, wonderful and full of divine insight! *IMAGINE* provides the 'missing link' in Christian understanding and practice between the natural and the supernatural realms that many believers have been seeking for years. Dr. Barbie Breathitt has done the body of Christ a great service by providing a solid biblical foundation for understanding how the natural and spiritual interact—how we integrate that process into our own lives by cooperating with the Holy Spirit.

These books are both paradigm-changing and life-altering. It is a wonderful blend of contemplative and analytical biblical thinking, personal experience building and divine revelation that will provide earnest believers with a new blueprint for the kind of walk with God they have always yearned for.

I suggest you read these books slowly and thoughtfully, perhaps several times, because it redefines the normative Christian experience in many fundamental ways. As you train your senses (Hebrews 5:14) this way, you will find yourself thinking all things have become new for me now.

Joan Hunter
Author/Healing Evangelist
Host, TV Show *Miracles Happen*

Dr. Barbie Breathitt's book series *IMAGINE* is a timely message, as this is the hour that God is releasing creative thinking and solutions from heaven. These books will open doorways to anointed thinking and the ability to see in the Spirit. This will activate your ability to dream and create at new levels through the Holy Spirit. This series is grounded in sound biblical teaching and practical instructions of how to apply it to your daily life. It is not just for creative dreamers, seers or songwriters—it is applicable to all the gifts, especially in business and ministry.

Doug Addison
Doug Addison.com
Author, webcast *Hearing God Everyday*, podcast *Daily Prophetic Words*, and prophetic blog *Spirit Connection*

Perfect, absolute peace surrounds those whose imaginations are consumed with you (Isaiah 26:3 TPT). Our imagination enables us to envision the Invisible One and thereby, as Barbie wrote, '…to redesign the image of ourselves.' The imagination is uncharted territory for Christians. We need more people like Dr. Breathitt to lead the way.

Ron Campbell

In her *IMAGINE* series, Dr. Barbie Breathitt's intensity of personae invites readers to partake in her deep insights, advanced levels of understanding and supernatural operations of faith in the glory realm. She challenges us not only to dream but also dares us to courageously imagine the impossible. Barbie creatively inspires us to unlock our potential in Christ through our imagination, to transcend the limitations of the flesh and progress in the limitless dimensions of God's glory.

I was often labeled as and teased about being a fantasizer during my childhood years, which greatly stifled the use of my imagination. The *IMAGINE* series has now unlocked the door to my imaginativeness, allowing me to freely and confidently advance. I have been awakened to the vast dimensions of God consciousness and His power, which equip me to exist and operate far beyond my God-given anointings and giftings. This series empowers me to live my future in the now!

Michael Adeyemi Adefarasin
Kingdom Lifeline Apostolic Ministries (KLAM), Abuja, Nigeria

A new era has dawned for God's people! A newfound season of supernatural revelation is being released from heaven to those who have the spiritual eyes and ears to see and hear what the Spirit is doing and saying (see Revelation 3:22).

Dr. Barbie Breathitt's *IMAGINE* series issues a clarion call for Believers to arise and supplant the old nature and attain their new identity in Christ. She implores readers to take on the very nature of Christ. She encourages them to utilize their divine imagination to create and decree their God-purposed destinies into reality in the same way God imagined and created before the beginning of time. Readers will discover the fundamental knowledge of how to apply their infinite imagination to shape their individual lives, influence the world and execute God's purposes.

Allow Barbie's *IMAGINE* series to transform your mind and usher you into a higher dimension of the Lord's destiny for your life!

Barbara Wentroble
President, International Breakthrough Ministries (IbM)
President, Breakthrough Business Leaders (BBL)
Author, Releasing the Voice of the Ekklesia; Becoming a Wealth Creator; Council Room of the Lord (series)

Works by the Author

Angels in God's Kingdom

Dream Encounters: Seeing Your Destiny
from God's Perspective

Gateway to the Seer Realm: Look Again
to See Beyond the Natural

So You Want to Change the World?

Hearing and Understanding the Voice of God

Dream Seer: Searching for the Face of the Invisible

Dream Interpreter

A to Z Dream Symbology Dictionary

Volume I Dream Symbols

Volume II Dream Symbols

Volume III Dream Symbols

Action Dream Symbols

When Will My Dreams Come True?

Dream Sexology

Sports & Recreation Dream Symbols

IMAGINE

REVEALING THE MYSTERIES OF GOD

Dr. Barbie Breathitt

VOLUME 1

IMAGINE: Revealing the Mysteries of God

Breath of the Spirit Ministries, Inc.
P.O. Box 1356
Lake Dallas, Texas 75065
BarbieBreathitt.com
BarbieBreathittEnterprises.com
DreamsDecoder.com

ISBN-13: 978-1-942551-05-8

9 781942 551058

Published by: Barbie Breathitt Enterprises, Inc.

Printed in Canada.

Dr. Barbie L. Breathitt

Dedication

It is my deepest honor to dedicate my series of five *IMAGINE* books to my best friend, personal confidant and beautiful baby sister, Brenda Doreen Breathitt. She was born in Lakeland, Florida on October 29, 1966 and transitioned into Heaven on Saturday, September 7, 2019 at the age of fifty-two. Brenda was a brilliant light of joy with an excellent sense of humor that caused us all to laugh. Her warm, inviting smile disarmed people, letting them know she was a safe place to share their hearts. Brenda was clothed with grace, compassion and beauty that sprang up from a deep well within her loving heart. Her caring concern for others exuded from her countenance to bless all those who knew her. Brenda was full of godly strength and dignity.

Brenda's name meant *the glory of God's sword. Let all who seek You rejoice and be glad in You; and let those who love Your salvation say continually, let God be magnified* (Psalm 70:4). She laughed and loved well through her painful battle with cancer knowing in the days to come she had a home in heaven. Her thoughts and prayers were with her unsaved friends and family members that she was leaving behind. She spoke with wisdom and godly counsel always carrying faithful instruction on her tongue. She diligently watched over her family, friends and household never eating the bread of idleness. Her only daughter Chelsea arises to call her blessed. There are many women who do noble things, but Brenda's loving nature, quick wit, sterling character and integrity surpassed them all. We all know that charm is deceptive, and physical beauty is fleeting; but I praise Brenda for she was a woman who feared the Lord. Those who had the chance to know Brenda honor her memory for all that her hands have done. No matter where Brenda went she always found a friend. Her sweet words of comfort bring her praise from the city gates. Brenda blessed so many in her life with unconditional love, a listening ear, and words of encouragement, profound humor and a shared smile. Brenda made all of us better people for having known her. She is sorely missed.

Barbie

Thank You

A special thank you to heaven's Prophetic Poet Keat Wade for sharing the amazing poems he has authored in his four amazing books: *For Whom Beyond Beckons, Dueling Kingdoms: Chronicling the Times, A Gnarled Tree and Me,* and *Chronology of Love: Times and Seasons.* All of his incredible poems are available on Amazon. com and through Christian Publishing Xulon Press.

Keat Wade's poems are unique in three ways, (1) the supernatural way poems are received (2) the visual of what is going on in the supernatural realm (3) and being in sync with God's Timing (Hebrew Calendar). Keat Wade shares intimate conversations with the Almighty. He only writes what he hears. Keat hears or visually sees either the title or the first line. Nothing more comes until he starts to write. Then the words flow in poem form as a divine download, complete in one setting. Keat feels drawn into that supernatural realm until the words are complete. Then it lifts. The poems reflecting the Timing of God picture what God is doing in the supernatural realm, thus giving confirmation or direction.

Keat is a graduate of Fort Hays State University. He is a writer by desire and academically prepared with a Bachelor of Arts degree in English and Speech and a Master of Education degree in guidance and counseling. Keat retired from his teaching at Oklahoma Wesleyan University. Keat and Judy Garlow Wade now live in the San Diego area where his prophetic writing began.

Foreword

God is restoring our vision with provision.

Dr. Barbie Breathitt's *IMAGINE* series persuasively inspires Believers to embark on a journey of self-discovery, seeking and finding God and to discover His hidden, concealed mysteries through their sanctified imagination.

Readers will be immersed in God's truth and transformed by fresh revelation, soundly based on Scripture, crucial to this new season of operating in supernatural strength, powerful influence and Christ's authority. One is introduced to the aspects and mighty functions of the Holy Spirit, the Seven Spirits of God, God's communication conduits (dreams and visions) and how to use the awakened imagination to pray effectively, tap into unlimited favor and blessings, access healing and manifest miracles.

This is a new day of opportunity. Our divine imagination affords us the ability to know and receive all that God has destined for us to be and accomplish. It is time to increase and expand our borders. Barbie's writings challenge us to disconnect from the religious, legalistic ways of reasoning and exchange them for the creative, life-giving mind of Christ.

These volumes stir us to imagine the impossible, to consider how we think, what we believe and how we relate to God Almighty and others so that we can become Christlike, accurately discern God's plans and purposes and manifest His glory for His Kingdom advancement. Barbie has managed to successfully use applicable Scripture-based examples and captivating stories throughout the series to enlighten, encourage and guide us through a spiritual conversion of our identity that empowers us to apprehend our extraordinary future.

Our God-designed, ingenious imagination births visions of the unknown things of God and brings the invisible realms of creation into focus so it can become a reality in our lives. What we create and see in our imagination causes us to encounter and experience a broader dimension of God.

God's Spirit is advancing and positioning us through the use of our divine imagination to equip us with wisdom, revelation, fresh anointings and unlimited prosperity in order to draw the lost, sick and dying unto Christ.

Dr. John P. Kelly
Convener, International Coalition of Apostolic Leaders
InternationalCoalitionofApostolicLeaders.com

Contents

IMAGINE: Revealing the Mysteries of God

Introduction

This book is the first in a series detailing how God desires His Beloveds to use their amazing, Spirit-filled imagination to *IMAGINE* their highest destiny, believe, see and manifest His glory on earth. My goal in writing these volumes is to help you gain a conscious awareness that the ingenious, creative Spirit of Christ Jesus dwells within the imagination of every born-again Believer. With this awareness and the awakening of the imagination, you will be able to understand the mysteries of God, set and actualize the clear cut goals about what you dream, prophesy it into existence and develop a plan to manifest the prophetic words spoken over your life—allowing you to fully achieve your desired destiny. The sky is not the limit; it's just the beginning!

I was attending one of Cindy Jacob's Apostolic Council of Prophet Elders in late 2018 when the Lord spoke to me. The following is a paraphrase of what He imparted:

> My prophets need to build Me a substantial platform that is large enough for Me to inhabit, to house and display My glory. My people keep postponing My coming, even with the terminology they use to praise and worship Me. Very few songs invite Me to come and display My greatness or declare the power and authority of My presence in the Now.
>
> My prophets prophesy—there *will* be a time coming, IAM

getting ready to, a new season *will* begin or in *two years from now* this or that will happen. When My prophets prophesy in this manner, because I honor the words of My prophets, I cannot manifest in a NOW way. I want to manifest My glory in the NOW!

I am limited to only manifesting in measure because of the small platform they build Me with their restrictive, futuristic words. I want My people to begin to exaggerate My Word so that I can begin to enter into and expose My grandeur with a NOW word of faith. My prophets are worried that if they prophesy a NOW word, I will not come, or it will not happen. Their fear of embarrassment restrains Me. But My Son, Jesus, became of no reputation. He only did what He saw Me (the Father) doing. I want My prophets to speak what they hear Me saying and do what they see Me doing on a grander scale.

He then brought me to passages in Ezekiel where God instructed him to command dry bones to come alive, to prophesy as He commanded (see Ezekiel 37).

When we prophesy as God commands, a certain sound is released, a shaking ensues and a coming together of One New Man occurs, and the Body of Christ resurrects out of the wilderness as a unified body that is full of power. God continues to call us to stop hiding, crouched in the corners, and to stand up in an elevated spiritual level of operation as individuals who are united as the Bride of Christ, having made herself ready to arise as One New Man.

In order to *see* what the Father is doing and to *prophesy* as He commands, we must operate in the expansive, spiritual fourth dimension, not the limited, worldly third dimension. We must transition from operating out of a gifting level into operating out of the glory level (see Revelation 4:5). Where we have normally operated in a gifting or anointing level, we are being called to step behind the veil into a mature level of Christ ministry, the Seven Spirits of God office level of fullness where all the limitations are taken off.

God is always communicating with us whether we are aware or not. God communicates to us through His multidimensional Spirits. The distinct dimensions of God's Spirits are: the Spirit of the Lord, the Spirit of Wisdom, the Spirit of Understanding, the Spirit of Counsel and Might, the Spirit of the Revelation Knowledge of Christ and the Reverential Fear of the Lord. All seven dwell within the Believer at varying degrees.

God created a specific system of communication for each individual person, a personal vocabulary depending on how one interprets. He speaks in puns, parables and symbols. When the disciples asked Jesus why He spoke in parables, Jesus explained that symbols had been given unto them (us) to understand the Kingdom of God that is within the Believer. We are enlightened to perceive by God's symbolic language, whereas the world is confused by it (see Matthew 13:10–17).

God speaks in parabolic phrases, so that we can come into the knowledge of God (spiritual realm) through the Spirit of Understanding in order to gain wisdom to move in His counsel, to move in His might. Being born of the Spirit, the Word becomes alive to us. God can

God is calling us to rise up as the Sons (and Daughters) of God in order to manifest His glory.

now speak to us through the Word, symbols, visions and dreams (see Job 33:14). He finds different and distinctive ways to speak to each one of us, and He does not speak the same way every time. God is very diverse (the multi-faceted wisdom of God).

Understanding God's symbolic language is possible through the expansive capacity of the imagination. The creative ability of the imagination is the conduit so to speak. God wants us to engage the imagination (the greater platform), so He can enter into it and express Himself in a much grander way to us than just by knowledge or by intellect. The imagination brings in the creative dimension God wants to use, so that He can express Himself to each person individually and to meet our specific needs.

I will highlight and explain various symbolic messages found in the bible throughout this and additional volumes, because if one can understand the symbolism of God, he or she can understand the mysteries of God. Consider God's symbolism as a tapestry. Each specific color of thread (a symbol or shape) communicates something distinctive, yet when each is joined or connected together, they form a unified pattern or image (revelation). If you take each aspect of that tapestry, tie it together and step back to observe, you will be able to see the big picture.

On a side note, this book and its subsequent counterparts are a continuation of my previous writings comprised of how to assemble the pieces of a symbolic puzzles in order to gain an understanding of God's love language, that empowers us to interpret dreams and visions that lead to our destiny. While it is certainly beneficial to have background knowledge of God's symbolic language unveiled in my other books, especially *A to Z Dream Symbology Dictionary* and *Dream Symbol Cards*, it is not necessary in order for you to understand the concepts revealed in these writings. You may refer to my other books at any time (listed in the back) for reference and better understanding.

The imagination empowers us to live and experience life in a much grander way. When we learn to live by our imagination, we will live life in abundance, in the best and the worst of times. The creative use of our imagination causes us to aspire to reach our full potential. By accessing God's supreme power, knowledge and wisdom through the Holy Spirit, we have the ability to operate as God designed us. By gaining the understanding of God's mysteries concealed in the soul of our thoughts and spiritual dreams, we can live in the future dimensions of increase. Accepting God's increase prepares us to step into and then steward the magnitudes of His multiplied blessings.

> The ingenious, creative Spirit of Christ Jesus dwells within the imagination of every born-again Believer.

We know God as our Creator by becoming an heir of Jesus' divine nature. The divine nature of God gives us the power to create things (in and through the imagination) not currently seen or known to exist. Resting in the divine nature of God causes us to imitate God by electing and agreeing with a prosperous future. There are many futures God has designed for us. Futures-in-waiting already exist in the realm of the Spirit for our imaginations to discover. We have the power to choose which destiny we will fulfill in life.

God is calling us to rise up as the Sons (and Daughters) of God in order to manifest His glory. This is only possible with faith. Faith is a master key that creates and unlocks our internal doors and spiritual gateways. It is one thing to have faith *IN* God; it is another to have the faith *OF* God. The plane of faith and the degree of godly character we master determines the depth, height, width and breadth of the future we will decide to demonstrate.

As partakers of the divine nature, we release God's powerful activities in and through our lives.

Faith defines the levels of God's grandeur we will choose to exhibit in our life.

> *So that they should seek the Lord, in the hope that they might grope for Him and find Him, though He is not far from each one of us; for in Him we live and move and have our being, as also some of your own poets have said, "For we are also His offspring." Therefore, since we are the offspring of God, we ought not to think that the divine nature is like gold or silver or stone, something shaped by art and man's devising. Truly, these times of ignorance God overlooked, but now commands all men everywhere to repent* (Acts 17:27-30).

As partakers of the divine nature, we release God's powerful activities in and through our lives. God's boundless love and infinite intelligence dwells in the heart of those who believe in the reality of Jesus Christ as their personal Redeemer.

The Father of Glory comes to awaken us to a new day of opportunity. The Holy Spirit opens the eyes of our understanding, and we are spiritually enlightened. When we are born again, godly revelation empowers us to see how to enter into the Kingdom of God in order to prosper and to fulfill all that God has purposed. No one can enter the Kingdom of God (which is within), unless they activate their childlike imagination in order to see, believe, perceive and accept the Kingdom of God (see Mark 10:15). Believers are endued with the power of influence, authority and a commanding sway of godly presence. We are called to reveal the mysteries of God that have been concealed within the hope of Christ.

The futuristic visions that Christ projects within the Believer's imagination shows him or her how to operate in the riches of God's glory. Everything we could ever want, need or desire is eternally stewarded in the realm of glory. When we take on God's glorious image and likeness, we become part of His glorious inheritance.

> *That the God of our Lord Jesus Christ, the Father of glory, may give to you the spirit of wisdom and revelation in the knowledge of Him, the eyes of your understanding being enlightened; that you may know what is the hope of His calling, what are the riches of the glory of His inheritance in the saints* (Ephesians 1:17-18).

The word *understanding* in the above passage is the Hebrew word *bin*. It means to go before time has happened, to ascend into the future realm of the Spirit in order to see the plans God has to prosper us, so that we gain a godly understanding to correctly interpret and apprehend the future. If we, as Believers of God, are able to enter the future to believe, see and understand the plans of God before they happen, we will be called upon by the kings and presidents from every nation of the world to boldly advise them from the wisdom found in the council chambers of God. *The Gentiles shall come to your light and kings to the brightness of your rising* (Isaiah 60:3).

The love of Christ Jesus dwelling in the imagination is the creative force that empowers us to access, know and surpass all the natural knowledge of this world. When we become aware that we are being filled with all the fullness of God, we are then able to gain understanding from another higher, more advanced spiritual dimension in God. The various attributes of the Seven Spirits of God are all unique master keys that give us entrance into the Father's many mansions (states of being) of God's Kingdom. When the truth of Christ's unlimited presence dwelling within us is actualized in our spirit man, we are able to live life in an exceedingly abundant state of prosperity.

We have been given access to the mind of Christ, to see Him for who He truly is, to know His full capacity and to obtain a broader dimension of the future. Tapping into the imaginative, creative, all-knowing mind of Christ gives us the ability to gain the supremacy of wisdom to move above and beyond all that we can ask, think or even imagine. As this new era dawns from the womb of the morning we arise as one mighty army that shines in the beauty of holiness. God is our strong tower of defense in the day of trouble. The kingdom of God, and the power of His Christ has come. We have been given the power to prophesy the heavens shut, so that no rain falls. In this day of His power, we freely volunteer to cast down the accuser. Our songs of deliverance declare God's power and mercy echoing throughout the earth then rises as a triumphant crescendo to the heavens.

Take a moment to IMAGINE what it would be like to live in a perfect world. A beautiful, tranquil world that is full of love. A world where everyone is at peace, full of love for their family and friends, and they care for their neighbors as themselves. A world where no one thinks evil of anyone much less intentionally harms another. IMAGINE a world where the furious lion and the innocent, gentle lamb lay down together in harmony. IMAGINE a world that functions under God's covenant law where people only do unto others as they would have people do unto them. IMAGINE a world where the thoughts and actions of people are always positive, kind, merciful and full of God's grace. IMAGINE a world that is free of hatred, prejudice, violence, disease, destruction, war and death. IMAGINE a world where people have the divine mind and Spirit of Christ dwelling within their being. IMAGINE all of the people in the world from every nation, race, tribe and tongue living together in one accord, freely worshipping the One True God in the Spirit of unity and in Truth.

IMAGINE being part the solution, the person who has the answers to all of the questions. IMAGINE being the person who brings salvation, peace and prosperity to the world. IMAGINE knowing God's voice, understanding the mysteries of God and being able to interpret dreams, visions and all mysteries. IMAGINE having access to all knowledge, all wisdom and all power in order to solve all of the world's problems.

Jesus, the Savior of the world, has all power and all authority both in heaven and on earth. He went around doing good and healing all who were oppressed by the devil, for God was with Him. Jesus gave His Believers power and authority over all demons and the power to cure diseases. He imparted His power to trample on serpents and scorpions and over all the power of the enemy, so nothing by any means can hurt you. Believers receive power from the Holy Spirit's presence, coming in and upon them, to be witnesses to the resurrection power of Jesus, to demonstrate signs, wonders and miracles of His great grace from one end of the earth to another. Jesus raised up Believers so that He may show His power in us, so that His name may be declared in all the earth.

The God of hope fills the Believer with joy and peace in believing that we may abound in hope by the power of the Holy Spirit. All Things are lawful for us, but not all things are helpful. All Things are lawful for us, but we will not be brought under the power of any, for Believers are submitted to the power of and controlled by the Holy Spirit.

Believers are seated with Christ in heavenly places far above all principality, power, might and dominion, and every name that is named, not only in this age but also in that which is to come. All Things were created by God that are in heaven and on earth, both visible and invisible, whether thrones or dominions or principalities or powers. All Things were created through Christ and for Him. The Believer is complete in Christ, who is the head of all principality and power. Believers should pray always that our God would count us worthy of this calling, so that we can fulfill all the good pleasure of His goodness and all the works of faith can be demonstrated with His power. God has empowered us to be His ambassadors here on earth.

Believers are called to demonstrate God's power, while being the brightness of His glory and the express image of His person. We are to uphold All Things by the Word of His power. Jesus had by Himself purged us of our sins, then He sat down at the right hand of the Majesty on High. His work is finished. Now we are called to manifest His Kingdom here on earth. Our prayer should be, "Lord, thy Kingdom come, thy will be done here on earth as it is in heaven!" For our God is able to do exceedingly and abundantly above all that we, the Believers in Christ, can ask, think or IMAGINE, according to the measure of our understanding of the power of God that works in us. The all-knowing, omnipotent God strengthens us with all might, according to His glorious power, for all patience and long-suffering with joy. In order to be Believers in Christ, we must be conscious of Christ's Spirit working in and through us.

CHAPTER ONE

Christ Consciousness

The Spirit of Christ is God-inspired consciousness; the ingenious and powerfully productive, creative energy force who skillfully imagined then spoke as He designed, formed and crafted the universe. As a result, Christ consciousness exists throughout the entire universe. Nothing was created, nothing exists and nothing holds together except in and through Christ. From before the foundation of the world, the great love of God chose each and every one of us as His very own to live the abundant life in Christ. His desired destiny for us is to be adopted as the children of God, holy and set apart as His blameless Beloved.

God created our body with the capacity to transcend time, space and eternity in order that we would be able to freely enter into God. Our body contains three life paths: the flesh, the soul and the transcendent spirit. Our spirit is the highest and only pathway that connects us to God. Scripture teaches that Jesus is the Son of God. Jesus Himself is God, and Jesus is the only access to God the Father. *I am the way, the truth, and the life. No one comes to the Father except through Me* (John 14:6). Jesus did not say He is *a* way or *one* of the ways to God. He said He is *the only* way to God!

The way to God is not a path trodden by men's feet. The way to God is by discovering, accepting and intimately knowing the essence of the person of Jesus Christ. Jesus is the living, powerful *Rhema* Word of God. Jesus contains all of the mysteries that are written within the Logos. Jesus imagined, designed and structured all of creation. He created the entire ever-expanding universe. Jesus uniquely fashioned each of our individual bodies and gave each of us exclusive, irreplaceable, rare gifts and diverse, distinctive personalities through which to manifest His manifold, multidimensional glory.

To become Christ-conscious and to operate as such, one must be born again of both Spirit and water to awaken the human spirit from death. By consciously receiving Christ as our Lord and Savior, His divine Spirit causes us to arise from the dead, as if awakening from a spiritual dream in sleep. The loss of life is a state of deep sleep. There is no transformational power in death, but there is unlimited, revolutionary power in eternal life. In death, our spirit is at eternal rest in the presence of the Lord while our physical body is waiting for the day of its transformation and resurrection. The Holy Spirit calls to us from within: *Awake, you who sleep, arise from the dead, and Christ will give you light* (Ephesians 5:14).

When we are spiritually awakened from the sleep of death, the Spirit of Christ comes in and dwells within us. We are no longer bound to the earth; we are able to ascend or translate into the heavenly realms. We have access to the mind of Christ, the power of Christ, the authority of Christ. Anything Christ has, we have; we become joint heirs with Christ. Christ consciousness is the ability to access the wisdom and the power of God, so we can become Christlike (a Christian). And until we become the wisdom of Christ, the mind of Christ, the power of Christ (Christ-conscious), we fall short of being a powerful representation of the living Christ for the sleeping world to behold.

Every good thing and perfect gift comes down from the Father of Lights in whom there is no variation or shifting shadow. By the exercising of His will, Christ brought us forth by the Word of Truth, so that we would be a kind of first fruits among His creatures (see James 1:17-18). Just as it was God's divine will to appear in person, riding on His Merkavah while shrouded in a brilliant, blinding light, to convert Saul in a vision. The divine Spirit chose to set Saul apart to be Paul, making him His loyal, steadfast, apostolic messenger of Jesus Christ. After Paul beheld the blinding brilliance of God's glorious light realm, his natural sight had to be restored. God sent His obedient servant Ananias, one who understood the voice of the Spirit, to pray for the scales to fall off of Paul's eyes.

The world has never been in a more desperate place. We need the bright light of God's presence to invade this present darkness with His universal, symbolic love language to give us His revelation knowledge. God's grace comes to bring His enlightening Spirit to give the Believer the spirit of peace,

God is calling us to awaken the Christ who is within us, because it is the Christ in us that gives us the hope of stepping into the glory realm.

unity and harmony and to lead us into His unmerited favor. God's favor resting on Believers brings us into the blessing of every spiritual gift that resides in the heavenly realm.

Christ redeemed, delivered and saved us through the power of His blood for the remission and forgiveness of all of our sins, offenses, shortcomings and trespasses. Therefore, we are born from above, putting on God's righteousness that is beyond reproach and we are able to rest in the riches of His generous love.

The Christ within us is exalted far above all rule, authority, power or dominion. He is above any name or title that can ever be conferred not only in this present age and this world but also in the ages and the worlds that are to come. Because God has already placed All Things under His feet, All Things are also under the feet of Believers unified in Christ and centered in His will.

God has appointed Christ to be the universal, supreme Head of the Church. What is more, Christ has chosen to exercise His headship through the blood-bought Church. The multiplied millions of Believers make up the one living Body of Christ, the great cloud of witnesses in heaven and on the earth. The combination of all of our gifts and faith working together in unity forms the full measure of Christ, the One who makes everything and everyone complete with Himself. Christ holds the whole world together (see Ephesians 1).

Jesus Christ is the divine, imaginative light of the world. The love of Christ Jesus empowers us to walk in the conscious awareness of His saving light.

Through the increased awareness of the Spirit of Christ living boldly within us, we express a greater degree of Christ's consciousness, grace, strength and power. A new day dawns within our lives as the Christ in us emerges and gives us more and more celestial light. The amount of heavenly enlightenment our soul possesses determines the level of godly wisdom, divine spiritual understanding and the amount of influence and physical success we experience in life. When Christ's light saturates our soul, we have the capacity to choose to rise to a higher state of being to become the light of the world. A city that is set on a hill that cannot be hidden (see Matthew 5:14).

The imagination is a life-directing force. The places and mansions that we create and see in our imagination cause us to experience profound events for the first time. This practice causes us to be proficient in the exercise of the desire to remain there in a higher place and to experience a broader dimension so that we become familiar with the ins and outs of navigating these encounters.

-A Choice-

A transport into worlds
Yet to be explored,
On subtly distracting pathways,
Broad and misleading,
Or, into spectrums of focused,
Well-designed corridors of light,
Maximizing the view of His path,
Prepared for our finding –
. . .To be explored eternally!

Keat Wade 05/06/19 (1 Iyar 5779)

Christ's light shining in and through the Believer causes him or her to be highlighted, promoted and favored. Like Esther, who chose to take the path less trodden and waltzed into the king's corridor and won the favor of all, we are called, chosen and set apart for divine purpose. The Christ within us emboldens our spirit to believe for the impossible. We must realize that those who consider something to be impossible is only their mistaken opinion.

Christ ignites our faith, so that we move in great faith. We are enabled to discover and trust in God's powerful, transcendent ways. The more we trust, the more we allow God's love and grace to flow through us. As God's love flows through us, the gifts flow and eternal fruit is produced based on the foundation of His love. The world witnesses this and is drawn to the loving Christ within us. When at rest in Christ (Christ-conscious), we shine and lift Him up, thus drawing all men unto Him.

As Believers in Christ, we do not deny the present condition of this fallen world. Instead, we understand that God's love shining forth from within our spirit is the guiding beacon of Christ's healing light to the world.

> *Then Jesus spoke to them again, saying, I am the light* (conscious awareness) *of the world. He who follows Me shall not walk in darkness, but have the light of life* (the inspired, conscious awareness of Christ; the eternal, brilliant light and life force of God)" (John 8:12).

We are called to project God's saving grace and revelation knowledge to the outer world. The knowledge of God comes so that others can be saved from the darkness of hatred, prejudice and death, so they can be awakened, resurrected and can live a transformed life in the ever-expanding Kingdom of God's Light.

God asked Job if he understood the mysteries of God: Where is the way to the dwelling of light (see Job 38:19)? Believers in Jesus exist in God's Kingdom of Light! God has opened heaven's communication lines. God reveals the hidden realms of mystery, so we can glean a deeper understanding of spiritual insights. Do you know where God's light dwells and

The way to God is by discovering, accepting and intimately knowing the essence of the person of Jesus Christ.

how to access it? We discover and access an increased measure of God's light and outshining as we arise in Christ consciousness.

Our true identity has been birthed to be both concealed and revealed in Christ. When our spiritually enlightened eyes look through the magnifying lens of our imagination, we begin to realize and quickly understand how all of the gifts, anointings and glory realms work together to advance the Kingdom of God. Believers are enlightened to the glorious abilities God has placed within us. *The eyes of your understanding being enlightened; that you may know what is the hope of His calling, what are the riches of the glory of His inheritance in the saints* (Ephesians 1:18).

God's grace gives us the understanding of how to become part of His glorious inheritance by becoming one of His saints. It is God's great pleasure for the Believer to know and understand how to apprehend the immeasurable, unlimited and surpassing greatness of His power that is resting dormant within. Our belief in Christ releases His power in us, so that we may demonstrate the working of His mighty strength.

> *Learning to dwell in the active, life-giving power of Christ consciousness causes us to be centered in God's perfect will.*

God's resurrection power raised Christ from the dead and seated Him at the right hand of God in heavenly places. Christ is also resurrected and living in the Believer. Christ rules the earthly Kingdom of God from within the enlightened eyes and Spirit-filled hearts of His Believers' imaginations. And at the same time, Christ rules the heavenly Kingdoms of God from His majestic throne in heaven. It is profoundly life-changing when one is fully cognizant of the truth that Christ lives bilocated in the soul of the Believer's imagination and at the right-hand throne of God.

Mature Believers are God's heritage; we are the Bride of Christ and are called to manifest as the Sons of God, uniting as One New Man! When we agree with the designs of God's counsel and will, we evolve into more of Christ's likeness in order to fulfill His purposes. When we are in Christ, we hear His voice of Truth. The Spirit of Christ dwells within our imaginations, so we can know His truth, believe Him for it and adhere to His salvation. God's promise of the Holy Spirit seals us with a guarantee of our being the first fruits of His inheritance. The presence of God within causes the Believer to anticipate the wholeness of redemption in order to acquire and possess God's fullness manifesting in his or her life.

In accordance with Christ's good pleasure, He has lavished His gracious favor and His divine, insightful wisdom and understanding upon us. Christ's Spirit reveals the secrets and mysteries of God's will, the plans He has for each of us to accomplish. His purposes are made known to us through our the illumination of our imagination.

Through a focused period of time spent in silent, deep imaginative thought, meditating on God's perfect will for our life, we are able to acknowledge and comprehend the Spirit of God at work in our life. God foreknew when the fullness of time would mature to bring forth the climax of the ages. Those who have placed their unending hope and confidence in Christ can celebrate and praise All Things in heaven and on earth that cumulate in Christ to the praise of His glory.

God is calling us to awaken to the Christ who is within us because it is the Christ in us that gives us the hope of stepping into and accessing the glory realm. Until the awakening occurs, we are relegated to staying in an anointing or a gifting realm. God's original intention and purpose was for us to move into the Spirit and remain in the realm of glory just as Adam and Eve walked with God in the Garden of Eden (see Genesis 3:8; 5:22, 24; 6:9; 48:1).

The work of Christ dwelling within us is there to reveal the way to God and the divine ways of God. His manifested truth is a light that guides us on the highest spiritual pathway of life. The Father grants us access to Jesus in the realms of glory. In the dimensions of God's glory, we gain spiritual insights into His vast wisdom. The spirit of revelation gives us access to understand the mysteries and secrets that are found in a deep, intimate knowledge of Christ. God floods the eyes of the heart (imagination) with His celestial light, so that one can discern and know the hope of His calling.

God has now disclosed and made known to us the mystery of the riches of Christ Jesus' glory that is resident within the Believer. Where this mystery had been hidden for ages and generations, it is now revealed to those who believe and diligently seek God with all their soul, heart, mind and strength of their imagination (see Colossians 1:26–27). The level or degree of conscious understanding we possess of Christ, the Anointed One, who died and rose to life again within us, determines the magnitude of the power of Christ's presence working in us that we can recognize, manifest and display.

The illuminating light of God's love dispels darkness to offer creative, inspired spiritual sight. God's radiant vision gives the imagination the ability to see. Just like Saul being blinded by God's light, true revelation knowledge gives us vision like the Apostle Paul to see God's eternal truths. The level of God's imaginative consciousness we have become aware of, searched out, gained the understanding of and experienced determines the measure of spiritual enlightenment that we are able to possess and utilize in our lives.

> *The Spirit of Christ dwells within our imaginations, so we can know His truth, believe Him for it and adhere to His salvation.*

When the spiritual eyes of our heart (imagination) are enlightened by God's Spirit, we instantly become aware of answers for which we have been seeking and waiting. Life's answers have always been patiently anticipating our discovery of Christ's all-knowing presence within us. Discerning the presence of the Spirit of Christ consciousness within endows us with the ingenious, creative force that is essential in order to speak every solution into existence.

The Holy Spirit also empowers our spirit to recognize, perceive and know the comings of the Spirit of God and to identify the goings of the Lord's presence. Jacob awoke from his sleep, and said: *Surely the Lord is in this place, and I did not know it* (Genesis 28:16).

To change our present state of being, it is essential to take our focus off of what was and that which has hindered and left us unfulfilled or dissatisfied. Jesus asks each person, "Who do you say that I AM?" The convictions you hold about God and yourself in Christ directly determine what you display in life.

Being acutely aware of Christ in us makes All Things possible. *You shall also decide and decree a thing, and it shall be established for you; and the 'Or' light of God's favor shall shine upon your ways* (Job 22:28).

God created in us a natural desire to decree and process something that we desire into existence. In addition to being consciously aware of its actuality, we must take on its image and likeness. Jesus said it this way: *If I be lifted up, magnified and exalted to a place of consciousness in your heart, I will draw all men unto Me* (John 12:32). No one is able to come to Jesus unless His Father draws that person to Him, for Jesus and His Father are One! To be like God, we must also become one with Christ to grow up into all of His ways.

Therefore, the Father is the state of consciousness (in which the Believer dwells) that draws to us the manifestations of the things we desire in life. When we desire Jesus, the Father draws us unto and then into Jesus.

> *No man has ever seen God at any time; the only unique Son, or the only begotten God, who is in the bosom in the intimate presence of the Father, He has declared Him. He has revealed Him and brought Him out where He can be seen; He has interpreted Him and He has made Him known* (John 1:18).

You must sanctify your consciousness to rise upon Christ until Jesus becomes tangibly touchable or real within you. It is the Christ in us that gives our spirit the ability to discern and consciously feel, see, hear and become a spiritual being that perceives His presence and speaks for Him. For no one can serve two masters; he or she will love the One (Christ) and despise the other. When we are aware of our right state of being (in Christ) and believe it to be truth (the Spirit of Truth) we will manifest that reality (Christ consciousness). By taking on the candor of that attitude, we mirror that particular *mansion* or state of being in our life.

A mansion is a large, stately dwelling place or house. The English word *manse* was originally defined as a property large enough for the parish priest to maintain himself. *Manor* is derived from the same root and denotes a territorial holding granted to a lord who would remain or dwell there. When I speak of a mansion, I am referring to a spiritual dwelling place, a state of being, an attitude, habitual action, personality or place of habitation in which we live, dwell, contemplate or spend most of our time. A mansion, therefore, is a higher plane, a different attitude, a different thought process.

It is taking on a new identity. We move out of old, narrow, habitual ways of thinking and confessing. When we take on the mind of Christ, we begin thinking higher thoughts. This moves us out of one mansion or state of being into a higher one.

In Scripture, we are called the Body of Christ, temples, houses or dwelling places for the Lord. Jesus went to prepare a superior place (mansion) for us. The mansion to which He referred is not just a future place of residency in heaven for us to inhabit after we shed our earthly bodies. It is where Christ is—in a higher state of spiritual existence and being. It is amazing that when we are conscious of Christ dwelling within us, we can dwell there too.

Jesus makes all of His decisions with His Father (who exists in a higher, divine spiritual state), the One who sent Him, so His testimony is reliable and valid. King David made it a habit to inquire of the Lord. He worshipped before Him until he could advance into a new state of being, attitude or territory (see 1 Samuel 23:2, 4).

> *"I am One of the two bearing testimony concerning Myself;* *and My Father, who sent Me, He also testifies about Me."* *Then they said to Him, "Where is this Father of Yours?" Jesus* *answered them as He stood in the temple treasury, "You know* *My Father as little as you know Me. If you knew Me, you* *would know My Father also." Jesus said, "I am going away* (into a higher state or mansion), *and you will be looking for* *Me* (by natural means of man's laws, traditions or knowledge), *and you will die in under the curse of your sin. Where* *I am going* (into the spiritual mansions of heaven), *it is not* *possible for you to come in your current carnal, mental state.* *You are from below* (natural, earthly and sensual; your spirit has not been born again or awakened from the dead)*; IAM* *from above* (spiritually alive, eternal and heavenly)*. You are* *of this world, of this earthly order; IAM divine, not of this* *world* (IAM from a higher realm, a heavenly kingdom of mansions)*. That is why I told you that you will die in and* *under the curse of your sins; for if you do not believe that IAM* *He Whom I claim to be—if you do not adhere to, trust in and*

Dr. Barbie L. Breathitt

rely on Me, you will die in your sins" (John 8:15–24).

Jesus told us that He was going to His heavenly Father, so that Believers could do greater works than He manifested on earth. When we learn how to go into the mansion that Jesus has gone before to prepare for us, we will emerge as the Bride of Christ joined to the Son of God, united as One New Man. In that spiritual mansion, we will do the greater works He foretold. *Most assuredly, I say to you, he who believes in Me, the works that I do he will do also; and greater works than these he will do, because I go to My Father* (John 14:12).

If the greater One is dwelling within us, orchestrating the visions that cross the screens of our hearts (imaginations), we cannot help but see how to manifest His greatness here on earth as it is in heaven. *For the Father loves the Son and shows Him All Things that He Himself does; and He will show Him greater works than these, that you may marvel* (John 5:20).

When the Believer awakens to the reality that Christ dwells within his or her imagination (Christ consciousness), he or she is empowered to accomplish miraculous feats. This is why the Bible declares:

> *It is impossible for those who were once enlightened, and have tasted the heavenly gift, and have become partakers of the Holy Spirit, and have tasted the good word of God and the powers of the age to come, if they fall away, to renew them again to repentance, since they crucify again for themselves the Son of God, and put Him to an open shame* (Hebrews 6:4–6).

Learning to dwell in the active, life-giving power of Christ consciousness causes us to be centered in God's perfect will. The peace of God gives us access to the Holy Spirit's revelation knowledge. The symbolic language of prayer, dreams and visions open the window of revelation that is from another future realm of time, which allows us to reach inside eternity to retrieve godly wisdom. When we discover how to access and understand God's revelation, His knowledge becomes an open gateway. God's wisdom freely flows from eternity, reaching into the temporal realm of time, to bring about and display His divine perspectives.

CHAPTER TWO

Man's Minds and Dueling Natures

It is necessary to understand the functionality of the conscious (Jesus Christ, the Son of God, Father) and subconscious (Father God) minds in order to adequately explain the dual natures of man and to fully realize other related concepts explored in this book and additional writings.

Through prayer, the conscious part of man's mind (knowledge) must tell the creative subconscious mind (who we are) exactly what it wants to manifest or which goal we desire for it to accomplish. One must have very specific goals so faith can stay strong and focused on accomplishing that prerogative. For example, if you are praying for or desiring the perfect mate, be specific while listing the characteristics, nature, personality, height, weight, profession and attributes that you desire when you alert your imagination to develop and draw the perfect person of your dreams. Now continually thank and praise God for answering your prayer. Then keep your eyes on the prize of the high calling of God. Keep visualizing your desired goal until your dream of a prince charming or a beautiful princess materializes and comes true.

> *No man has at any time yet seen God. But if we love one an-*
> *other, God abides lives and remains in us and His love that*
> *love which is essentially His is brought to completion to its full*
> *maturity, runs its full course, is perfected in us (1 John 4:12)!*

The three different parts of man are comprised of spirit, soul and body. The first is the internal, eternal spirit of man. Man's spirit is composed of the Spirit of Wisdom that gives us the ability to commune with God in spirit and in truth. The second is the soul. The soul is the carnal nature or personality of man. It is comprised of the mind and all its mental, intellectual capacities, memories and the desires of our determined will and our emotional, feeling components. These components make up the inner workings of the soul's desires.

It is the spirit and the soul that ultimately battle for supremacy.

The third is the outer, natural part of us; the physical body that safely houses our spirit, soul and internal organs. It is the spirit and the soul that ultimately battle for supremacy.

We use both our physical and our spiritual senses to educate us on the visible and invisible worlds surrounding us. The conscious, objective mind is the reasoning, logical part of the mind. This is where we make our choices and decisions as well as develop our personal belief systems based on what the information that the conscious mind searches, gathers and draws through the five physical senses. This is done by learning or education, by observation or by experience. The wise person focuses on manifesting the positive things they desire, not on the negative difficulties of life.

The subconscious, subjective mind is the creative force or the seat of our emotional intelligence that perceives through our spiritual intuition without using any of the natural senses. It keeps our automatic bodily (respiratory, digestive, nervous and circulatory) systems functioning without cognizant thought. The subconscious seeks the Lord Jesus.

> *When I needed the Lord I sought, looked and inquired of Him. Of a necessity, I called out to Him on the authority of His Word. He heard me, responded and delivered me from all my fears. He rescued me from everything that made me so afraid* (Psalm 34:4).

Believers must remember that God did not give us a spirit of fear but of love, power and a sound, Christ-centered mind. The subconscious uses our spiritual gifts to gather revelatory insights. Although the subconscious mind is always receptive to the thoughts and plans of the conscious mind, it is ultimately the greater of the two. *My Father,* (subconscious) *who has given them to Me, is greater than all; and no one is able to snatch them out of My Father's* (subconscious) *hand. I* (Christ-consciousness) *and my Father* (subconscious) *are One* (see John 10:29-30).

To amply illustrate the relationship between the conscious (the creative Christlike) and the subconscious (Father) imagination, I will refer to each as masculine (he) conscious and feminine (she) subconscious imagination respectively. The conscious mind basically tells the subconscious imagination what's what. The subconscious imagination does not argue with the conscious reasoning mind; she submits to and believes whatever the conscious tells her. Whatever is imprinted on or instilled into the imagination, she willingly receives, incubates and creates bringing it forth into manifestation She is, in essence, a womb, the creative aspect of what is communicated to her. The subconscious takes whatever the conscious tells her and gestates, nurtures and protects it, grows it and produces it, essentially bringing it to life.

> *The carnal man responds or reacts to external factors of the flesh that are at enmity with the spirit and are continually at war against God and His knowledge.*

Jesus Christ announced, *"Nothing I do is from My own initiative, I* (consciousness) *can do nothing of Myself, for as I hear the judgment passed by My Father* (subconsciousness), *I execute judgment. And My judgments will be perfect, because I do not seek My own will, I* (consciousness) *can do nothing on My own, except to fulfill the desires of My Father* (subconsciousness) *who sent Me* (John 5:30)."

The subconscious does not debate truth; her truth is whatever has been dictated to her. For example, if she is told the moon is purple, she believes the moon is purple. She is like the foot soldier who receives orders from her strong, confident general (conscious). She does not question the validity of or the reason for the orders. She simply receives the orders and begins to *imagine* how to carry out the orders effectively. The subconscious needs to be inventive to do or generate what the conscious has communicated.

The imagination exists and operates in the womb of the subconscious, ultimately being one in the same.

> *Jesus asked His disciples, "Have you been with Me all this time, and you still don't understand? To see Me is to see the Father. Don't you believe that the Father is living in Me and that I am living in the Father? The words that I speak to you aren't My own. They are not mere words but they contain His spirit and life. I don't just make them up on my own. The Father who resides in Me crafts each word into a divine act to perform His miracles of power through Me"* (John 14:10).

We often think about the things we imagine and the actual things we perceive as being detached and separate. However, the conscious and subconscious (imagination) work together as one. *Are you greater than our father Abraham (physical man), who is dead? And the prophets are dead. Who do You make Yourself out to be (John 8:53)?*

Just as the conscious directly impresses the subconscious, the subconscious, in turn, unequivocally shapes the conscious to influence our behavior and existence. It is an endless circle of cause and effect. What we imagine, the thoughts that emerge or are birthed, alter our actual perception (consciousness). Our reality or our being is then changed. In short, the consciousknowledge we possess imprints on the subconscious. The information or knowledge that is imagined, is then enhanced, grown and produced by the subconscious or imagination. Once this occurs, the conscious acknowledges the process is complete, and then we are able to take dominion, rule, reign and replenish the earth as God's stewards.

God spoke:

> *"Let us make human beings in Our image, according to Our likeness; make them We will make them a reflection of Our nature. Mankind will have dominion and be responsible for the fish of the sea, the birds of the air, and over the cattle, over all the earth itself and over every creeping thing on the earth. God created human beings; He created them godlike, reflecting God's nature. He created them male (conscious) and female (subconscious). God blessed them: "Prosper! Reproduce! Fill*

Earth! Take charge! Be responsible for fish in the sea and birds in the air, for every living thing that moves on the face of Earth (Genesis 1:26). "

What we become consciously aware of comes to us from within our imaginative subconscious. Accordingly, we and our reality become of what we are conscious. *For we can do nothing against the truth but for the truth* (2 Corinthians 13:8).

As an example, if our conscious believes that someone does not like us, our subconscious will meditate on that input until we anticipate their avoidance. Our conscious perception of their dislike will cause us to sabotage ourself by subconsciously acting in destructive ways, which will insure that they will sidestep, elude or continually reject us. The subconscious acted on and fulfilled within itself what the conscious mind thought by mirroring the information it received in real life.

We subconsciously manifest what we think and believe. The Bible commands us to meditate and dwell on true, noble, pure, positive, good, well-pleasing things (see Philippians 4:8). Once we decree and focus on the end result of that decree, it will manifest and be established in our life.

God has given us the art of prayer so that we can join our faith to retrieve the possibilities found in the imagination. So we can learn to deny what is in our physical, outer senses to accept and believe what is already accomplished in our inner desires. For prayer to cleanse, change and recreate our subconscious thoughts to obtain a higher spiritual life expression, there must be no conflicting opinions. Focus on the end result of what God has destined you to be. *We are of God, when we enter the Kingdom of God as little children, trusting God with all of our heart to overcome the world: knowing that greater is He that is in us, than he that is in the world* (1John 4:4).

After learning the workings of the conscious and the subconscious, it becomes clear how imperative it is that we search, gather and draw from the spirit, not the carnal negative reasoning mind, to manifest Christ, not the lust of the world. As Believers, we recognize that the only true reality is Christ consciousness.

As specified, man has both physical and spiritual senses. The natural man has five senses by which to navigate his environment, but he is spiritually dead (see Ephesians 2). Therefore, his spiritual senses are also dead or dormant. The natural man, who is dead in the trespasses of sin, is separated from God. The natural man does not see or place any relevance in God. The carnal man responds or reacts to external factors of the flesh (sin, worry, anger, fear, jealousy); they are at enmity with the spirit and are continually at war against God and His knowledge.

The spiritual man who is born again also has five natural senses, but he is led by his higher spiritual senses that hear, see, taste, feel and smell invisible things as well. In fact, the book of Hebrews tells us that our spiritual senses grow by being exercised by the reason of their use.

A fitting example of the difference between physical and spiritual senses is when Jesus was almost physically crushed by the crowd on His way to heal Jarius' daughter. Jesus made no mention of or comment to any specific person who physically made contact with Him *until* a suffering woman touched the hem of His garment. By touching only the edge of his cloak, not Jesus' body, the woman was instantly healed. Jesus said, "Someone touched Me; I know that the power of healing virtue has gone out from Me" (see Luke 8:42–46). Although Jesus could physically feel many pressed against Him in that moment, He could also spiritually feel when the faith of one particular woman drew healing power out from Him.

She knew what she wanted, and she set her heart (imagination) to obtain what she desired! She activated her faith by repeatedly telling herself, "If I can only touch the hem of Jesus' garment, I will be healed!" She repeated this healing mantra so many times that she believed in her own healing declaration. The hearing of her own inner voice and then decreeing those words out loud caused faith to arise within the center of her being. She had imagined herself healed and saw herself whole again. She pictured herself fighting her way through the press of the crowd. She imagined how it would feel as she reached up and grasped Jesus' tallit at the end of His prayer shawl. The woman who had been infirmed with an issue of blood for twelve years imagined she would be healed at the point of contact. Her focused faith saw, felt and experienced her miracle before it took place. She knew she would be healed through reaching out, and with one touch of the Master, her life would be restored.

Dr. Barbie L. Breathitt

In the same regard as senses, there are two major forms of vision or worldview. One is from the natural, subjective, biased, carnal, prejudiced conscious mind of man whose reality is ruled by the dictates of the world, the one-sided, five physical senses of what is appearing in the now. The natural, personal senses blind us by restricting our vision to only being able to see the present, earthly realm of existence. *But the natural man does not receive the things of the Spirit of God, for they are foolishness to him; nor can he know them, because they are spiritually discerned* (1 Corinthians 2:14).

The other form of vision is from the Spirit. To *see* in the Spirit, we must disengage from the subjective generalities of the world and stop relying on our physical senses. To do this, we must develop our visual acuity by totally relying on the Holy Spirit and the accuracy of our keen spiritual senses. By concentrating our focus upon the invisible, we receive the gift of visionary sight. *For since the creation of the world, His invisible attributes are clearly seen, being understood by the things that are made, even His eternal power and Godhead, so that they are without excuse* (Romans 1:20).

> To see in the Spirit, we must disengage from Egypt's subjective, worldly generalities and stop relying on our physical senses.

Supplanting the Carnal

We are continually confronted with our dual natures that war with one another for dominion. The sinful attitudes of the carnal natural man always battle with the enlightened spiritual man for control. These conflicting dual powers of the will collide within the womb of our being and produce a sharp clash as each struggle to emerge as the firstborn, dominant victor.

This battle is effectively unveiled in Scripture with the story of Jacob. To make the narrative more comprehensible, I have included the meaning of names here: Isaac (laughter, child of promise); Rebekah (bound, refreshed); Jacob (benevolent supplanter, represents the spiritual part of us that receives God's promises); Esau (hairy, strength, represents the outermost part of our carnal appetites and the strength of our fleshly being); Laban (white, glorious); Haran (parched, dry); Beersheba (well of the oath).

One nature is represented by soft, tent-dwelling, Spirit-seeking Jacob. The contrasting character is earthbound, carnal, fleshly-motivated Esau the wild hunter. Esau functions from his natural senses to determine facts. He lost God's favor when he willingly sold his birthright as the firstborn son to satisfy his ravenous appetites and depraved hungers. He traded his leadership mantel for a pot of beans to satisfy and strengthen his weary flesh. Every day we are confronted with the question: Will we be led by the Spirit's divine nature, or will we yield to the wild hairs that cover the strong arm of our fleshly appetites?

Esau represents our soulish personality before it is born again. *But Esau I have hated, and laid waste his mountains and his heritage for the jackals of the wilderness* (Malachi 1:30). To please God, we must learn to put our natural, fleshly ways to death. We must supplant or replace our firstborn, natural man (Esau) with the smooth-skinned, spiritually intuitive man (Jacob). Jacob went through the imaginative transformational process. Jacob wrestled with God to emerge as a Prince. *As it is written, "Jacob I have loved, but Esau I have hated"* (Romans 9:13).

When we desire something immediately, the fleshy Esau engages our primitive nature. He loads his sharp, piercing words (weapons, bow and arrows) and departs to hunt, to take captive by force the object of his desire. Esau is even willing to control, assassinate, use slander, gossip or kill something in order to satisfy his appetites and gain whatever it is he desires. As we mature, the spiritual Jacob who communes with the Holy Spirit (mother Rebekah) learns to move into a place of favor with the Father's (Isaac's) blessing by supplanting the first nature (Esau).

Abraham, the Father of Faith, begot Isaac, his long-awaited promise. Isaac was forty years old (The number forty means: a mighty mass of water like the deep; to come from the water downstream; many things in chaos; a period of probation; a testing of conduct, character and trials; chastisement of covenant sons; closing in victory, revival and renewal; defeat or judgment; generational completed rule; a generation of man; the history associated with salvation.) *when he took Rebekah as his wife. Isaac pled with the Lord for his wife Rebekah, because she was barren; and the Lord granted Isaac's plea and she conceived twin boys.*

Rebekah, Isaac's wife, conceived. But the children struggled together within her; and she said, "If all is well, why am I like this?" (If I have been born again why am I still struggling?) *So, she went to inquire of the Lord. And the Lord said to her: "Two nations* (opposing natures) *are in your womb, two peoples* (differing belief systems) *shall be separated from your body; one people shall be stronger than the other, and the older* (natural man, Esau) *shall serve the younger* (spiritual man, Jacob)." *So when her days were fulfilled for her to give birth, indeed there were twins* (dual, antagonistic natures) *in her womb* (Genesis 25:19–24).

Jacob's father Isaac was very feeble and almost completely blind. Isaac tried to discern between his sons, Jacob (the spirit) and Esau (the flesh), by using his own dull, physical senses.

Isaac was old and his eyes were dim so that he could not see. Isaac called Esau his elder son to him and said, "My son! I am old, I do not know when I may die. So now, I pray Esau, take your weapons, arrows and bow, and go out into the open country and hunt game for me. Prepare the meat the way my appetite loves it and bring it to me, that I may eat of it, in preparation for giving you my blessing as my firstborn son before I die."

Isaac's wife Rebekah overheard their conversation and sprang into action. She was determined to get the blessing Isaac intended for Esau as a blessing for Jacob. Rebekah prepared two goats, dressed Isaac in Esau's clothing, covered his hands and neck with the goatskins and instructed Jacob to take the meal to his father.

And Isaac said to his son Jacob, "How is it that you have found the game so quickly, my son?" And he said, "Because the Lord your God caused it to come to me." But Isaac said to Jacob, "Come close to me, I beg of you, that I may feel you (natural touch), *my son, and know whether you really are my son Esau or not."*

So, Jacob went near to Isaac, and his father felt him and said, "The voice is Jacob's voice, but the hands are the hands of Esau." Isaac could not accurately identify Jacob by using his physical senses, because the goat skins made Jacob's hands feel hairy like his brother Esau's hands; so, Isaac blessed Jacob. But Isaac said, "Are you really my son Esau?" Jacob answered, "I AM." Then Isaac said, "Bring it to me and I will eat of my son's game, that I may bless you." Jacob brought it to Isaac and he ate; and Jacob brought Isaac wine and he drank. Then his father Isaac said, "Come near and kiss me, my son." So, Jacob came near and kissed him; and Isaac smelled Jacob's clothing and blessed him and said, "The scent of Esau my son is as the odor of a field which the Lord has blessed. And may God give you of the dew of the heavens and of the fatness of the earth and abundance of grain and new wine; let peoples serve you and nations bow down to you; be master over your brothers, and let your mother's sons bow down to you. Let everyone be cursed who curses you and favored with blessings who blesses you."

After Jacob (the spirit) *received Isaac's spiritual blessing* (the promise) *of prosperity, thus supplanting or replacing Esau* (the flesh), *Jacob fled Beersheba and departed toward Haran to stay with his mother's brother, Laban* (Genesis 27:1–29).

Blind Isaac relied on his feelings and physical senses of touch and smell to lead him to know or discern who to bless. Isaac's firstborn Esau also depended on his natural, physical strengths. These canal natures oppose the spirit as they reside in the womb or soul of every person.

In the invisible spiritual realm, our inner man of imaginative thought and spirit takes on a face and form so that he or she appears tangible. There our desires have substance and weight that displaces atmospheres in order to make room for themselves.

There are additional examples in Scripture where we see the principal of the spiritual man replacing or supplanting the natural man just as Jacob replaced Esau: Jesus Christ, the spiritual man of God, replaced John the

Baptist, while He carried the same message of repentance; Elisha replaced or supplanted Elijah by doing twice the number of miracles; David, the spiritual worshipper of God, supplanted or replaced King Saul, a man whose height and physical stature was celebrated.

> When we utilize our sanctified imagination, meaning it yields and is fully submitted to Christ, we are not accessing our carnal thoughts, plans or purposes; we are seeing what the Father is doing.

Similar to the account of Esau and Jacob, Tamar's story in Genesis 28 illustrates the effects of Judah, like Isaac, being led by the physical senses as well as the spirit supplanting the carnal during the birth of their twins.

Tamar (means *palm tree; victorious spirit;* see Micah 5:9) was originally the wife of Er (means *an aroused, excited wild ass; to accumulate and strip*) the firstborn of Judah (Praise). After her husband's death, Tamar was given to Judah's second son Onan (means *to experience much trouble or vigor*) who also died (neither Er nor Onan were willing to bring forth children, so God took them). Not understanding the ways of the Spirit and fearing the loss of yet another son, Judah sent Tamar back to her father instead of offering her his third son with whom she could have children (to possess her promise).

After some time, Judah's wife passed. After his grieving period ended, Judah went up to Timnah (forbidding) where his men were shearing his sheep. Tamar was determined to obtain the inheritance (a child from his line) that was promised to her. When she heard of Judah's plans, she took off her widow clothes (the past), covered herself with a veil (new identity) and positioned herself at the entrance to Enaim (a rare, dual, open place where two ways meet; entrance to two fountains or springs; two eyes), which was on the way to Timnah.

When Judah saw Tamar, he thought she was a prostitute. Because he was led by his natural, carnal senses, he did not realize she was his daughter-in-law. Judah offered to send her a young goat in exchange for her services. In her prudence, Tamar required something as a pledge of his promise. Like Esau, in his haste to fulfill the desires of his flesh, Judah gave Tamar his seal and its cord and his staff. Tamar became pregnant with twin boys by him (one son for each of her previous husbands) and returned to her hometown.

Three months later, Judah was informed that Tamar was guilty of prostitution and pregnant as a result. Judah demanded she be burned to death for her actions. Tamar sent a message to her father-in-law asking if he recognized the seal and staff. Judah's (spiritual) eyes were opened, and he said, "She is more righteous than I, since I wouldn't give her to my son Shelah (means *sprouting petition*)."

As Tamar was giving birth, one of the twins put out his hand. The midwife immediately tied a scarlet thread to his wrist signifying he would be the firstborn. However, when he drew back his hand, his twin brother came out first. Tamar named the twin who was born first Perez (means *breakthrough*) and the second Zerah (means *rise up and shine*). Perez (the spirit) supplanted his brother (the flesh) and seized the firstborn birthright before he took his first breath.

Personal Reflection Moment

1. Take a moment to evaluate in what areas you may need to shift from using your physical senses to using your spiritual senses.

2. Are there times perhaps the carnal man has more command over your thoughts and actions than the spirit man?

As we exercise the spiritual sensations of our imagination flowing through our divine gifts, they mature, gain strength, expand and ascend into a higher realm of discerning, glory and function. If the inner man and the higher function of the spirit pilot us, we will not follow the destructive compulsions of the lust of the flesh.

CHAPTER THREE

The Imagination

The subconscious imagination is who a person is, what he or she does and how he or she behaves. It is made up of the hidden, subliminal parts of us. And it is exceptionally intuitive. Scientists have proven and measured the light that shines while the brain is in the process of recording waves of mental and emotional vibrations during thoughts, dreams and visions as well as during the physical actions of others beyond our beings. This is what the bible refers to when it describes people being led by the luminous cloud of glory by day and the brilliant pillar of fire by night. *See, I am sending an angel ahead of you to guard you along the way and to bring you to the place I have prepared* (see Exodus 23:20).

The imagination is able to discern the positive and angelic messages, sounds, anointings and the presence of glory as well as the negative energy fields of sin, sickness, disease and the vexing, draining vibrations of demons.

The five natural senses must be transferred into heavenly spiritual senses to break out of earthbound thinking and limitations in order to receive an awakened imagination.

The imagination is also able to discern the ether sound waves of thought in a person's mind. This capability enables the imagination to read and discover the intents of a person's motives.

Thoughts move like lightening when they are evolving within their being. People describe this ability (sensitivity to others' thoughts) by saying, "I have a hunch, knowing or feeling." This is commonly called *intuition*.

The power of imaginative thoughts is not encumbered by time or space. It has been documented that although twins, family members and soulmates may be miles apart from each other, they can still communicate with each other through imaginative thoughts. This is possible even if they are on another continent, separated by oceans or on a different geographic plane, hemisphere or in a different time zone. When a married couple is unified in the Spirit and in tune with each other's feelings, they are able to send loving thoughts to one another's minds without saying a word.

Imaginations create noble or ignoble thoughts. A sanctified or an awakened, Christ-centered imagination enables us to stay focused on things that are pure, lovely and holy. *I will refuse to look on any sordid thing; I will set nothing wicked before my eyes; I detest the worthless deeds of those who stray; I hate the work of those who fall away; evil will not get a hold on me it shall not cling to me* (Psalm 101:3).

The Lord is righteous in all His ways and faithful in all He does (Psalm 145:17).

For your ways are in full view of the Lord, and He examines all your paths (Proverbs 5:21).

When we utilize our sanctified imagination, meaning it yields and is fully submitted to Christ, we are not accessing our carnal thoughts, plans or purposes; we are seeing what the Father is doing. Believers who are leery of or opposed to using their imagination are often considering its use within an earthly or carnal realm. These uses include, but are not limited to: fantasies, lust-filled thoughts, telling untruths, intimidation, control, manipulation and exaggerations.

> We must have our mind renewed with the Spirit of Christ in order to take on the mind of Christ.

Those who use their imagination in this regard are operating in something that is evil or false, or they use the imagination for vain purposes and for their own promotion. Worldly or carnal knowledge used in this fashion is against God and is not profitable except that we acquire living-life experiences or learn something that increases our intelligence. *Again and again they limited God, preventing Him from blessing them. Continually they turned back from Him and provoked the Holy One of Israel* (Psalm78:41)*!*

A vain imagination produces images of fleshly desires that stir the fires of passion within our loins. *Wash yourselves, clean up your lives; make yourselves clean; put away every speck of the evil of your doings from before My eyes. Put an end to all your evil* (Isaiah 1:16).

Her priests violate My laws and desecrate and profane My holy things. They fail to distinguish between the sacred and profane. They no longer teach that there is a difference between pure and impure, the clean and unclean, the holy and unholy! They have hidden their eyes from Me completely disregard My Sabbaths; as a result, IAM defamed and profaned among My people (Ezekiel 22:26).

While you did these things, I kept silent; somehow you got the idea and thought that I was altogether like you; but now My silence ends, I will rebuke and indict you, I'll state the charge against you clearly, face to face, and set them in order before your eyes (Psalm 50:21).

The Lord detests those whose hearts are perverse (imagining immoral corruption and creating fantasy)*, but He delights in those whose ways are blameless* (Proverbs 11:20).

You can use your imagination for good and holy things to advance the Kingdom of God, or you can create vain imaginations for evil. Therefore, It is extremely important to guard the images you set before your eye gate. *For Your lovingkindness is always before my eyes, on my life's journey I have walked in Your truth down the path of life* (Psalm 26:3).

For example, if I asked you to imagine that you are holding a piece of hot pizza in one palm of your hand, you could feel the warmth on your skin and smell the hot, fragrant cheese and pepperoni (even though you are only imagining the presence of pizza). If I then asked you to imagine that you are holding an etched-glass bowl while eating an icy-cold ice cream sundae in your other hand, you could easily discern the changes in weight, fragrance, texture of the glass and temperature (even though the two subjective objects are not in your physical hands).

The five natural senses must be transferred into heavenly spiritual senses to break out of earthbound thinking and limitations in order to receive an awakened imagination. God is calling everyone to awaken to serve the true and living God with a conscious awareness of His presence. John 5:2–15 illustrates this calling with an account of one man's encounter with Christ:

> *There is a pool near the Sheep Gate in Jerusalem. This pool* (represents conscious awareness) *in Hebrew is called Bethesda* (house of mercy), *which has five porches, alcoves, colonnades and doorways* (these concrete gateways represent the five natural senses that only hear, see, taste, feel and smell earthly evidence).
>
> *In these five doorways laid a great number of sick folks* (unimaginative)—*some blind* (lacking vision, uninspired, ordinary), *some crippled* (traumatized, rejected, feeling invalid), *and some paralyzed* (fearful), *or shriveled up* (lazy, inactive)—*waiting for* (someone else to heal them) *the bubbling up of the water.*
>
> *For an angel* (messenger) *of the Lord went down at appointed seasons into the pool* (consciousness) *and moved and stirred up the water* (giving an idea, thought or message); *whoever then first, after the stirring up of the water* (conscious awakening of the imagination), *stepped in* (took action on the idea, impression or thought) *was cured of whatever disease with which he was afflicted.*
>
> *There was a certain man there who had suffered with a deep-seated self-pity and a victim's mentality. He thought he needed someone else to do something for him that he could do for himself. He had this lingering mental disorder for thirty-eight years* (thirty-eight means slavery; to break faith as a Harlot in her worldly, wilderness wanderings).
>
> *When Jesus noticed him lying there in his helpless state of being, knowing that he had already been a long time in that condition, He said to him, "Do you want to become well?"* (Are you really in earnest about getting well?) *The invalid* (made

an excuse or shifted blame onto someone else) *answered,* *"Sir, I have nobody when the water is moving* (opportunities that arise) *to put me into the pool; but while I am trying to come into it myself, somebody else steps down ahead of me." Jesus said to him, "Get up! Pick up your sleeping pad and walk!" Instantly the man became well and recovered his strength and picked up his bed and walked. But that happened on the Sabbath* (day of rest). *So, the Jews kept saying to the man who had been healed, "It is the Sabbath, and you have no right to pick up your bed, it is not lawful." He answered them, "The Man Who healed me and gave me back my strength* (an idea, the courage to try, health and vision for life)*, He Himself said* (prophesied) *to me, "Pick up your bed and walk!"*

We cannot relate to God through our fleshly intellect (what we know about God through our carnal mind). We must have our mind renewed with the Spirit of Christ in order to take on the mind of Christ. Then we can know Him through a spiritual knowledge that allows us to relate to God in His Kingdom, in His mansion. We can know Him through and relate to Him in the Spirit of Knowledge which comes from a heavenly realm. We can use our imagination because it has been sanctified. It's a pure thought, a holy thought.

When we use our imagination in this manner, we can manifest the greater works of the Kingdom of God. We are not using worldly knowledge or ways. Instead, our spirit has ascended into the kingdom of the heavens and has gained heavenly knowledge and heavenly wisdom. We have brought that imagination down into our bodies' earthen vessels, so it can gain entrance into the earth in order that His Kingdom comes and His will is done on earth as it is in heaven. The Spirit of Christ is now ruling in our heart and in our mind. Our mind has been renewed by the Spirit of Christ. We think higher thoughts, and we walk in higher, Christlike ways.

CHAPTER FOUR

Knowledge

The importance of imagination far exceeds the scopes of just knowledge, for the expanses of the imagination reach beyond the known world. Before we can fully explore the awakened imagination, we must become familiar with the different knowledges that the imagination uses and draws from, their definition and their significance.

Knowledge is defined as the fact or condition of knowing or being aware of something with familiarity that is gained through learning experiences, acquaintances or associations. It encompasses the range of one's learned information or level of understanding. Knowledge is the ability to apprehend truth and the principles or facts

> *Godly knowledge will lead and guide us to gain spiritual understanding.*

through reasoning abilities in order to gain intellectual awareness of unusual knowledge. Scripture clearly affirms God is the author and source of all knowledge, not man. *Talk no more so very proudly; let no arrogance come from your mouth, for the Lord is the God of knowledge; and by Him actions are weighed* (1 Samuel 2:3).

God desires us to seek and acquire knowledge. *The heart of the prudent acquires knowledge, and the ear of the wise seeks knowledge* (Proverbs 18:15). That being said, God desires us to seek His knowledge and wisdom first and foremost, not the world's. Knowledge comes when it is sought out and willfully discovered, while the wisdom we possess continually lingers in our presence. This relates back to the differing operations of the carnal Tree of the Knowledge of Good and Evil and the development of the spiritual minds found in the Tree of Life.

Worldly Knowledge

Worldly or earthly knowledge is considered to be the abbess, the place where the two-headed serpent bites. One head brings forth a positive change, to enhance and increase, while the other immediately devours by initiating the negative, destructive, prideful demise of man. Man fell from the Spirit realm and died when he chose to eat from the Tree of the Knowledge of good and evil. When man fell, the glory lifted from his body and man's eyes were opened to see through a cloudy, distored filter of sin; they were also turned inward to focus on self. Subsequently, all Adam could see and think about thereafter was his own naked depravity.

While the ingenuity of the imagination has no boundaries, its inspiration and inventiveness are likewise limitless.

All earthly knowledge must be steadfastly rooted in Christ's love in order that we do not become arrogant or haughty; pride enslaves us to deception. Paul taught that earthly knowledge puffs up, twists, controls and falsely distorts our perspectives and it destroys if it is not firmly grounded in the love of Christ. The love of Christ builds up, clarifies and edifies; it causes no harm.

> *For this reason I bow my knees to the Father of our Lord Jesus Christ, from whom the whole family in heaven and earth is named, that He would grant you, according to the riches of His glory, to be strengthened with might through His Spirit in the inner man, that Christ may dwell in your hearts through faith; that you, being rooted and grounded in love, may be able to comprehend with all the saints what is the width and length and depth and height—to know the love of Christ which passes knowledge; that you may be filled with all*

the fullness of God. Now to Him who is able to do exceedingly abundantly above all that we ask or think (imagine), *according to the power that works in us* (Ephesians 3:14–20).

Earthly knowledge absent of the love of Christ is self-serving to its own entity. It is insufficient, full of lust and unable to satisfy. It not only restricts the beholder, but it also impulses the beholder to dominate or yoke others yielding knowledge in a selfish love. For example, an arrogant person often aggressively rails and explodes into an irrational rage when he or she is not able to dominate others or control all of his or her circumstances. People who operate in haughtiness attempt to force others to comply with their ideology, will or personal desires and whims. If their anger cannot produce the needed fear to accomplish their objective, they resolve to skillfully creating a deceptive web to delude, sabotage and ensnare their victims.

You must be on guard to not allow the weaknesses in your personality or anyone else's to control or dominate you! Instead, invite the Spirit of God's presence and the essence of His truth to manifest, so that you can identify Holy Spirit's desire being birthed within you in order to bring forth a brand new, Christlike image.

Worldly knowledge is valuable, but it is limited to only what we currently know and understand. Natural man simply cannot create from what is not already known. Yet if knowledge is developed in a spirit of righteousness (positioned in right standing in God's ways) and amplified by our creative imagination, then that type of godly knowledge will lead and guide us to gain spiritual understanding that is only found in God's divine knowledge.

Above all things, God directs us to keep the Sabbaths. Being able to enter into a Sabbath rest with God is the sign He created between Himself and us for generation after generation in order to keep the knowledge alive that He is the God who makes us holy.

The imaginative, creative consciousness of God's light dwelling within us is more important than knowledge. The knowledge we possess is limited to the scope of what we presently know or understand how to produce. Therefore, we need to not only be aware of but also harness His divine light to press beyond our human margins. While the ingenuity of the imagination has no boundaries, its inspiration and inventiveness are likewise limitless. This arena of recognition is where All Things are indeed possible. *But Jesus looked at them and said to them, "With men this is impossible, but with God all things are possible"* (see Matthew 19:26).

Jesus said to him, "If you can believe, All Things are possible to him who believes" (see Mark 9:23). The godly knowledge we possess and the degree of faith we place in believing in God will determine the level of success we will experience in life.

Spiritual Knowledge

God places an extremely high value on the pursuit of spiritual knowledge. It is important to remember that spiritual knowledge is vastly different than academic knowledge. To know something spiritually, we must experience and live it for ourself. To obtain spiritual knowledge, we must be transformed into its image by taking on its likeness. We must become it in order to possess and reflect that attribute of Christ. To know something academically is to only hear or read about it and then compare another's thoughts or experiences to our own life experiences. We essentially listen to and analyze what other people tell us about it. This is great information, but it is only secondhand knowledge. Earthly knowledge is not transformational; only spiritual knowledge has eternal weight and fruitful consequences.

In order to encounter God and understand His ways, we must seek to embrace a spiritual change that is eternal. To be saved, changed, healed or transformed, a personal touch by the Spirit of God is required. Moses had his burning bush encounter. Saul met God's Merkabah chariot of light on the road to Damascus and was transformed into Paul. We encounter God, so we can build a relationship with God.

The Spirit of Knowledge gives life-changing revelation and is at the center of the five dimensions of creation. The first being the mercies of God that sustain us with hope; they are new every morning. Secondly, the justice of God empowers us to distinguish who and what is worth fighting for. Thirdly, the peace of God that passes all understanding unlocks us to receive revelation knowledge. Prophetic revelation speaks from the heart of God's perspective as revealed by the Holy Spirit. We are able to see the future as God sees it and to walk in His higher realms of reality and truth.

Dr. Barbie L. Breathitt

Fourthly, the victory found in God alone empowers us to be constant and persistent in our pursuit to discover the knowledge of the mysteries of God. Then lastly, the indwelling grace of the Spirit of God causes us to prosper and succeed in every area of life for eternity.

Sacrifices end in death, not life. But the sacrifice of Jesus forever changed everything. His resurrection steals life from death. Taking the keys of death, hell and the grave from satan make it possible for those who trust in God to offer their bodies—eyes, ears, mouths, hands, feet—to God as a *living sacrifice*. Believers become a sacrifice and yet live.

> *Brothers and sisters, in light of all I have shared with you about God's mercies, I urge you to offer your bodies as a living and holy sacrifice to God, a sacred offering that brings Him pleasure; this is your reasonable, essential worship. Do not allow this world to mold you in its own image. Instead, be transformed from the inside out by renewing your mind. As a result, you will be able to discern what God wills and whatever God finds good, pleasing, and complete* (Romans 12:1–2).

The Spirit of Knowledge is listed in Scripture as the sixth gateway (mansion) of light. When this spiritual gateway is open, it funnels heavenly revelation into us. Each of these seven individual, fiery gates mentioned in Isaiah and Revelation offer us access to a broader, more comprehensive and mature expression of who God is and how He operates in the Holy Spirit.

This allows us to shift from operating in a gifting level to an office level of fullness where all the limitations are taken off, and we step into a level of Christ ministry. We progress from a word of knowledge to the Spirit of Knowledge. We graduate from a word of wisdom to the Spirit

> *The Spirit of Knowledge gives life-changing revelation and is at the center of the five dimensions of creation.*

of Wisdom, from a word of counsel to the Spirit of Counsel and so forth.

The Spirit of the Lord shall rest upon Him, the Spirit of Wisdom and Understanding, the Spirit of Counsel and Might, the Spirit of Knowledge and of the Reverential Fear of the Lord (Isaiah 11:2).

Who, then, are those who fear the Lord? He will instruct them in the ways they should choose (Psalm 25:12).

I will instruct you and teach you in the way you should go; I will counsel you with My loving eye on you (Psalm 32:8).

Commit your way to the Lord; trust in Him and He will do this (Psalm 37:5).

Blessed are those whose ways are blameless, who walk according to the law of the Lord. They do no wrong but follow His ways (Psalm 119:1, 3).

Teach me, Lord, the way of Your decrees, that I may follow it to the end (Psalm 119:23).

Cause me to understand the way of Your precepts, that I may meditate on Your wonderful deeds (Psalm 119:27).

I have chosen the way of faithfulness; I have set my heart (imagination) *to think on Your laws* (Psalm 119:30).

As beneficiaries of Christ Jesus, Believers enter into God's creative abilities and divine structure to manifest God on earth. In God's glorious presence (seeing Him), we develop into His image. We understand how to access the glory to essentially seem believe and imagine to invent everything we need. By growing in the knowledge and ways of God's glory, we usher in the new eras of God to manifest Him in a broader, different and more profound manner. *And Hezekiah gave encouragement to all the Levites who taught the good knowledge of the Lord* (2 Chronicles 30:22).

Godly knowledge begets expansion. *Out from the throne came flashes of lightning and rumblings and peals of thunder, and in front of the throne, seven blazing torches burned, which are the Seven Spirits of God, the sevenfold Holy Spirit* (Revelation 4:5).

Godly knowledge grants us the spiritual insights necessary for us to have the upper hand in life, providing an advantageous edge. We become competent, clever and skillful in using our hands and imagination to advance into God's storehouse of infinite abundance.

Believers who have divine knowledge possess spiritual understanding and practice God's divine aptitudes become leaders; they have access to the unlimited mind of Christ, His wisdom and all that He knows. Men and women who possess divine knowledge are favored by God and man over others. They are chosen to lead depending on the degree of godly knowledge and integrity they possess. *So, I took the heads of your tribes, wise and knowledgeable men, and made them heads over you, leaders of thousands, leaders of hundreds, leaders of fifties, leaders of tens, and officers for your tribes* (Deuteronomy 1:15).

True knowledge can also come at a great price. Innovators, for example, are willing to suffer rejection and endure persecution in order to introduce others to a new, productive idea, a revolutionary discovery or to develop some cutting-edge concept. As it is with the natural, so it is with the spiritual. A higher degree of spiritual knowledge also comes with much suffering and persecution instituted by family members, friends or those who do not have the equal level of understanding. *And everyone who has left houses or brothers or sisters or father or mother or wife or children or lands, for My name's sake, shall receive a hundredfold, and inherit eternal life* (Matthew 19:29).

Who shall not receive a hundredfold now in this time—houses and brothers and sisters and mothers and children and lands, with persecutions—and in the age to come, eternal life (Mark 10:30).

To acquire real knowledge about Christ, we must be willing to unlearn and renounce what was taught to us by man. Like the innovator who discounts and releases others' not likely thinking or opposition to new ways of thinking, the obtainment of knowledge requires us to let go of falsehoods, erroneous thoughts and some traditional or false cultural beliefs. *That I may know Him and the power of His resurrection, and the fellowship of His sufferings, being conformed to His death* (Philippians 3:10).

Because we are justified by faith in Christ, we are enlightened to enter into a realm of supernatural peace. In this condition of peace, we become conscious of anything that may be warring against us or anything that may be causing chaos in our sphere of influence (people, circumstances, choices). We are then able to ask the Christ within to help us recognize or discern the root cause of the issue. In His grace and mercy, the Prince of Peace gives knowledge, wisdom and discernment to whomever asks.

When revelation comes as promised, everything unlovely that we have become passive about is realized. We must be careful not to be critical or judgmental of ourself in the midst of the illumination. It is for peace and freedom in Him that God exposes what keeps us in bondage. We need to simply repent of any known sins, renounce the embracing of a wrong belief and reject it. Then pray for the wisdom necessary to change what was previously believed.

As long as your soul continues to react to the rhetorical situations in your life as well as others' adverse responses with the very same damaging thoughts or actions, you will remain trapped in a destructive loop that generates the exact same cycles of undesirable responses. The remarkable grace of God brings salvation to all men. His grace teaches us to reject ungodliness and worldly, immoral desires and to live upright, sensible, godly lives that reflect spiritual maturity.

> *By growing in the knowledge and ways of God's glory, we usher in the new eras of God to manifest Him in a broader, different and more profound manner.*

Our truth is redefined and elevated when we break free of all the unlovely thoughts that defile us as well as the criticisms from others or even ourself that justify us living in the lower levels of existence. Embracing a higher, godly knowledge and truth empowers us to ascend another rung on a spiritual ladder to a statelier position. It is essential to agree and realign your thoughts with a larger measure of truth as you dwell in an advanced level of Christ consciousness.

We attract what we place our focus upon. Therefore, focus your attention on learning more about the loving, creative Christ within the imagination. How does one attain and maintain a proper focus to achieve this?

> *By doing all things without complaining and disputing, we become blameless and harmless, children of God without fault in the midst of a crooked and perverse generation, among whom we shine as lights in the world* (Philippians 2:14–15).

CHAPTER FIVE

The Knowledge of God

God gives us all the spiritual knowledge we seek after, but He also gives us *His* knowledge concerning all matters. We mature in the knowledge of God first and foremost by reading, studying and writing His Word on the tablets of our heart. We also develop in the knowledge of God through our own individual adventures with Him. The knowledge of God and accepting and moving in His love are vital to our sanctification and transformation.

Jesus established His essentialness to the Believer:

> *You shall know the Truth* (the living person of Jesus Christ; the logos and rhema Word of God that produces the image of God; the foundation of creation; the One who brings us into the center of God's purpose), *and the Truth shall set you free* (John 8:32).

Truth is not a fact of something we see, a statement or an insight. Truth is the divine person of Christ.

There is a natural course of happenings that occur as a result of pursuing and attaining the knowledge of God. We first gain an inner understanding of the presence of God that is dwelling inside our being. We then learn how to effectively contemplate the existence of eternal, spiritual things. By gaining the knowledge that God's Word produces, a firm foundation upon which we can build a new life, we are able to structure the principles and precepts of God within our being. After we have established the reality of God's presence dwelling within us as a life-changing force, we take on His image and likeness. Thus, by internalizing our knowledge of God, we can display His power externally.

We are given an example of an internal principal of truth when Jesus boldly stated:

> *I know who I AM. If I say, "I didn't know Him* (the Father)*"* *I would be a liar. Yet you have not known Him, but I know Him. And if I say, "I do not know Him," I shall be a liar like you; but I do know Him* (the Father) *and keep His Word* (John 8:55).

Do you know God as depicted in the above verse? Have you experienced His love, saving grace, mercy and healing salvation?

> *And we know that the Son of God has come and has given us an understanding, that we may know Him who is true; and we are in Him who is true, in His Son, Jesus Christ. This is the true God and eternal life* (1 John 5:20).

This is the core of the knowledge of God.

Have you ever asked yourself, "Who am I really in Christ?"

To discover our true identity, it is necessary to move away from focusing our attention on our own knowledge of our personality or temperament and direct our attention to the characteristics of Jesus. By relying on Christ and His attributes, we can emerge in a new way in order to manifest a changed identity that is centered in the essence of Christ who is within us. *I, wisdom, dwell with prudence, and find out knowledge and discretion* (Proverbs 8:12).

Wisdom calls aloud outside; She raises her voice in the open squares. God desires truth in the inward parts, and in the hidden part. You will make me to know wisdom. Who has put wisdom in the mind? Or who has given understanding to the heart? Incline your ear to wisdom, and apply your heart to understanding. The Lord gives wisdom; from His mouth come knowledge and understanding. He stores up sound wisdom for the upright. He is a shield to those who walk uprightly. He saw wisdom and declared it; He prepared it, indeed, He searched it out. When wisdom and knowledge enter your heart, it is pleasant to your soul. So, teach me to number my days, that I may gain a heart of wisdom. The mouth of the righteous speaks wisdom, and his tongue talks of justice. My mouth shall speak wisdom, and the meditation of my heart shall give understanding. Happy is the man who finds wisdom, and gains understanding; 'Behold, the fear of the Lord, that is wisdom, and to depart from evil is understanding.'

The level of our spiritual hunger (for the knowledge of God) determines the degree to which we discover the personal knowledge of ourself, our callings, abilities and core purposes. All of these attributes are meant to function harmoniously to fulfill the destiny for which we were born. Our personal, individual desires drive us to seek, know and understand God in order to discover our true selves. *Wisdom and knowledge are granted to you; and I will give you riches and wealth and honor, such as none of the kings have had who were before you, nor shall any after you have the like* (2 Chronicles 1:12). God's resident wisdom dwelling within His righteous Believers will draw the kings of this world to the light of our rising.

> *To acquire real knowledge about Christ, we must be willing to unlearn and renounce what was taught to us by man.*

Do you fully comprehend that the expansive, limitless Kingdom of God resides within you?

The knowledge of God travels outward from within the inner space of our being to manifest and to fill in the vast spaces of our world. Packaged with the infinite Kingdom of God comes the responsibility of exercising and managing its immeasurable power prudently. Carelessness kills; complacency murders. The tongue of the wise uses knowledge rightly; the lips of the wise generously disperse knowledge. But God gives us wisdom and knowledge as we come and go among the people of the world, so that we can govern well.

The knowledge of God working in our life empowers us to take dominion, to rule and to rein in our outer world through His righteousness. The measure of the truth of God we possess and understand determines our ability to properly utilize the power of God. To overcome the weakness of sin and death and to conquer the world, we must first know the person and power of Christ who is living within us. *The eyes of the Lord preserve knowledge, but He overthrows the words of the faithless* (Proverbs 22:12).

The God of heaven is to be greatly esteemed. There is both an objective (outside) heaven and a subjective (internal) heaven. We are surrounded by heaven and such a great cloud of spiritual witnesses.

God keeps our days secure and stable with His gifts of wisdom, salvation and surplus of knowledge. Therefore, we must let go of every wound and the sin into which we can so easily fall. When we cast off these impediments, we are competent to run life's marathon with passion and determination, for the path has already been set before us. *Let us throw off everything that hinders and the sin that so easily entangles. And let us run with perseverance the race marked out for us* (Hebrews 12:1).

Be diligent to collect God's counsel, and guard it with your life. Tune your ears to Wisdom; for her glory is better than great wealth. Make spiritual insight your priority, and its virtue will keep a watchful eye out for you. Set your heart on gaining understanding of the fear of the Lord. Knowledge is a pleasant companion who is guarded by God. It takes wisdom to build a mansion and understanding to set a house on a firm spiritual foundation. It takes knowledge to furnish our life with the beauty of holiness. Wisdom is a good friend and common sense keeps us from danger. The wise accumulate the true treasures of knowledge; their perceptive words flow from them like a clear spring of water.

Believers need to not only seek the knowledge of God, but it is a necessity to also ponder, pray about and properly steward the knowledge that God reveals to us during prayerful dialogues, meditations upon the Word and in the dream visions of the night season. You could begin with a simple declaration like, "Lord Jesus, teach me Your ways, so that my ways can be rooted and grounded in Your love."

The book of Psalms is peppered with brilliant affirmations to pray and meditate on. Psalm 119:66 offers an excellent example: *Teach me good judg-*

ment and knowledge, for I believe Your commandments. The Greek word knowledge in this verse is *gnosis*, which means the type of intimate knowledge that is discovered through sexual love between a husband and wife.

As the bible specifies, Adam knew his wife Eve intimately, to know yada sexually. Because we were made in His image, we can become intimate with the love of God and act just like Him. Marriage was designed by God to mirror and set an example of the intimate relationship He designed to have with us. Because they *know* one another so well, those in marriage covenant often take on the same attributes and mannerisms of their partner. With God, virtuous attributes are the only possible ones to mirror. Unfortunately, this is not so with people. We are also subjected to becoming intimate with the hateful influences of darkness even without being aware at times.

Jesus warned of this possibility and its consequences when He corrected James and John. He directed these sons of thunder that they must not know, discern, recognize or be aware of what kind of evil, destructive power they were both coming under the influence of. How often is this true about each of us when we wish someone harm or respond to someone in a hurtful, critical, angry or judgmental, negative manner? We will be judged by the same measure of hostile criticism that we spew toward others.

When negative thoughts and impressions are sent out toward others and received by them, we have placed them in bondage to our horrible, loathsome opinions. However, if they refuse to receive or they rebuke the vain imaginations we have projected on them, those very same, harmful impressions and curses that we imposed on them will return to bind or afflict us.

We know God with our heart by communing with Him in the realm of Spirit and Truth. Ecclesiastes 1:16 demonstrates this reality: *I communed with my heart, saying, "Look, I have attained greatness, and have gained more wisdom than all who were before me in Jerusalem. My heart has understood great wisdom and knowledge."*

Prayer and the dreams of the night carry us into the spiritual zones where access to the internal knowledge of who we are destined to become is granted. *Day unto day utters speech, and night unto night reveals knowledge* (Psalm 19:2). Let the visionary dreams of the night plan your days. Always embrace what your imagination determines is possible; excitement will explode in your life.

I ask God to commune with me, to teach me while I sleep on a regular basis, and I strive to write down what I remember from His visits as soon as I wake. If we do not give attention to record, to interpret and fully understand the messages of our dreams and the answers to our prayers, we will woefully miss the opportunity God offers us to discover who and where we are presently.

Without understanding our dreams, we can never become who we are destined to become in the future. Likewise, without the correct interpretation of our dreams, we may not obtain the full potential reserved for us, our destiny. The accurate understanding of our dreams helps us to properly see and know ourself, so that we may reach the full span of our prospective purpose.

If you are confused about or find yourself losing sight of what is important in life, permit your sanctified imagination to take the lead. The sanctified imagination will always bring matters back into an accurate perspective. To manifest anything you desire in life, simply dream and imagine it is there. When you awake, it is so!

Because we are created in God's likeness and image, we can tap into the reality of God's conscious, imaginative energy to encounter all the diverse dimensions of His creative, healing light that is found in Christ's divine power, wisdom and presence. God's powerful presence enlightens us. In His ever-increasing light, we receive and shine with His profound wisdom.

We behold the imaginative dreams and visions of God that give us the understanding of how to produce inventive ideas. If we follow the Holy Spirit's lead, we will find His abundant shower of prosperity. The visionary images we receive from God produce a symbolic awareness in us. When we are aware of something's existence, we are able to focus on understanding what it means and how to use and develop it until we can give it birth in the fullness of time.

As we learned, the conscious and the subconscious (imagination) interact interchangeably. Therefore, if a fact can produce a state of thought, it should also be possible for a thought to produce a physical fact or place. *Whatsoever things you desire, when you pray see them as an imagined reality, believing that you have already received them, and you will receive it as an answer to prayer* (Mark 11:24).

When we imagine something, we birth the seed of an idea. When we give that idea expression, we cause it to manifest in our mind's eye. The awareness of knowledge grows into maturity through understanding responsibility and gaining wisdom by experience. As long as they are joined to faith-filled actions, we are able to create anything through our God-given imaginations, dreams, visions, inspired thoughts, prayerful words, prophecies and decrees.

Imagination, A Place

Where You provide the thoughts
And inspired words flow
From this Spirited Pen,
Painting word pictures, supreme,
Seen as personal, individual, images
Through anointed eyes of the reader.

Keat Wade 05/15/19 (10 Iyar 5779)

As a born-again Believer, you have the limitless knowledge of God already residing inside of you. God Almighty loves to impart His knowledge to you, so that you may have His knowledge on All Things or about any matter in your life. God desires for you to know and discern what He's doing and why He's doing it.

Personal Reflection Moment

1. Do you actively seek the knowledge of God? Not just spiritual knowledge or the knowledge about Him?

2. Do you allow Holy Spirit the time to communicate His knowledge to you regarding personal and life matters? Or do you often pray about matters then proceed with your knowledge in hand?

CHAPTER SIX

Revelation Knowledge and Faith to Receive

Revelation is an act of revealing or communicating divine truth, something that is revealed only by God to humans. As Believers in Christ, we are given access to the mind of Christ to retrieve and utilize all of His wisdom, understanding and revelation knowledge. We need only ask to gain the understanding of godly knowledge. When we skillfully apply understanding or revelation, we can alter, amend and increase the scopes of our future events, because nothing is impossible with God (see Luke 1:37). *Our Lord is great. Nothing is impossible with His overwhelming power. He is loving, compassionate and wise beyond all measure* (Psalm 147:5).

Revelation knowledge allows us to travel in the Spirit to the place of God consciousness (where we discover the reality of Jesus). Herein lay the answers to all of our questions. Jesus is the door that opens for us to move into a higher mansion or state of being where He is seated with His heavenly Father. The *Way* welcomes and fully receives us.

A new or renewed desire for Christ causes our present state of consciousness to ascend by moving into that elevated, yearned-for state.

> *In My Father's house are many mansions* (states of consciousness, states of being)*; if it were not so, I would have told you. I go to prepare a place for you. And if I go and prepare a place for you, I will come again* (through answers to prayers,

dreams, visitations and visions) *and receive you to Myself; that where I AM* (in a higher state of being), *there you may be also* (John 14:2–3).

Faith is the power that opens God's revelatory gate. Our imagination, therefore, can draw out or extract answers and wise solutions that have been restrained in the realm of the Spirit. These answers and solutions have been patiently waiting for us to believe them into our present reality. *In Him you also trusted, after you heard the Word of truth, the gospel of your salvation; in whom also, having believed, you were sealed with the Holy Spirit of promise* (Ephesians 1:13).

The power of our belief releases the needed measure of faith to swing open heaven's doors wide enough for the wisdom of God (revelation knowledge) to flow out into our soul. As believers, we are charged to steward all the good things of the Lord here on earth. *Then Jesus said to the centurion, "Go your way; and as you have believed, so let it be done for you." And his servant was healed that same hour* (Matthew 8:13).

> *Our personal, individual desires drive us to seek, know and understand God in order to discover our true selves.*

Faith is the fundamental key to fruitful and effective prayer, to receive and understand divine revelation. Faith is required for our prayers to be seen, felt, heard and answered. Faith is essential for our prayer requests to be received by God; without faith, it is impossible to please Him. Steadfast faith and trusting in God's Word, promises and faithfulness is compulsory for the answers to be released from the Spirit, to be agreed upon, believed and ultimately realized by us. *Therefore, I say unto you, whatsoever things you desire, when you pray, believe that you receive them, and you shall have them* (Mark 11:24).

In order to receive something from God, we must know exactly what we want and how to ask for it. We ask in faith, already believing we have received what we have asked. Faith is a substance of something that is hoped for. To receive what we hope for, we must know what makes up the substance of our desire. Write your specific hopes down, and make them as plain as possible. Then state, pray, decree, declare or prophesy each desire as a clearly defined goal. Jesus asked the people He prayed for, "What do you want Me to do for you?" Do you know what you want from God?

Years ago, I needed a larger ministry vehicle that could carry my family and ministry team for road trips. I wanted a fully loaded, white Cadillac SUV with tan leather interior and carpet and captain seats that reclined for added comfort on long road trips. I didn't have the needed funds at the time. I started praying. I visualized what my new automobile would look and feel like when I rode and hauled resources, luggage and passengers.

Shortly after I imagined my new vehicle, I received an invitation to be a guest on Sid Roth's *It's Supernatural*. The product sales and ministry engagements from that TV appearance generated enough money to purchase the Escalade SUV of my dreams from an auction. People were dumping large cars because of gas prices, so there was a surplus from which to choose. The one I ended up with was even better than I had imagined. It had six captain chairs

> *Our imagination can draw out or extract answers and wise solutions that have been restrained in the realm of the Spirit.*

instead of four and an extended back end, which made hauling lots of books and suitcases very easy. God wants to do exceedingly, abundantly and above all we can ask, think or imagine.

When we pray, we must do so from a state of already envisioning ourself in the configuration we desire instead of ambiguously petitioning God for what does not yet exist in our imagination. We are directed to ask for anything in God's names, which means ask in prayer having assumed the same poiwer that is found in His nature, character and attributes.

> *You did not choose Me, but I chose, have appointed and planted you, that you might go and bear fruit and keep on bearing, that your fruit may be eternal and everlasting, remaining and abiding. So, that whatever you ask the Father in My name, as presenting a consciousness of all that IAM, He may give it to you* (John 15:16).

Here, Jesus is referring to asking in the nature of the fullness of the IAM consciousness of God and manifesting that desire. He is not referring to selecting any one of His hundreds of names in which to pray.

To receive what we ask for in prayer, we must assume that state of being in our person as a manifested reality. *And when that time comes to ask, you will not need to ask Me any questions. I tell you, that My Father will grant you whatever your ask in My Name* (presenting yourself in the fullness of the nature of IAM) (John 16:23). We must, therefore, assume the trait or attribute of the divine nature of God or the dimension that we are asking for in order to become it before we can receive the power that is contained in that actual, desired state. Everything we do must be from out of the new name "IAM" that God has given us, that is written on the white, glory stones. IAM who and what God says IAM. (I will elaborate on our new identity in Volume II of the *IMAGINE* series.)

The patiently waiting answers to our prayers are drawn to us by our imagination when we activate our measure of faith to become *now, godlike faith!* Now faith is the confident fidelity of the substance that causes the things that we hope for and trust in to form the strength of our relationship in the Person of God. Faith becomes a manifested substance of the evidence of things not seen that are brought out of the heavenly holding chambers. Now faith causes spiritual movement in our imagination, so that the answers to our prayers can rain down, freely fill up our being and pour into our current circumstances.

Our enlightened imagination enables us to ascend into the realm of great faith where miracles are conceived, birthed and instantly manifested.

> *But when you pray, go into your most private room, and, closing the door* (the awareness of your present form of being), *pray to your Father* (that awareness of being who you desire to be), *Who is in secret; and your Father, Who sees* (you taking on a new attribute of Christ's identity) *in secret, will* (acknowledge your changes) *reward you in the open. And when you pray, do not heap up phrases, multiplying words, repeating* (statements about your current, negative condition

or lack) *the same ones over and over like some mantra as the Gentiles do, for they think they will be heard for their much speaking. Do not be like them, for your Father knows what you need before you ask Him* (Matthew 6:6–8).

Shut the door on the old. Continue knocking. Stay focused on drawing what you desire until a new, Christlike image arises. Establish the evidence of your new conscious state of being in Christ with great conviction. Things appear in a new (subconscious) state of IAM, and they are transferred to us through the door of our consciousness.

God honors the spiritual principle that teaches us to be persistent in season and out of season. Preach the word! Be ready in season and out of season. Convince, rebuke, exhort, with all long-suffering and teaching (2 Timothy 4:2).

When the heart of our imagination is set on God, we will continue to tirelessly seek His face with a determined urgency. *And let us not grow weary while doing good, for in due season we shall reap if we do not lose heart* (Galatians 6:9).

We are told to *Seek the Kingdom of God first and His righteousness* (His way of doing things right), *and all these things will be added to us* (Matthew 6:33). When we are conscious of being in Christ, seek His Kingdom and do things His way, we have found the way, the truth and the life. At this time, we can decree a thing, and it will be established for us. The Spirit of the Lord instructs us to tirelessly ask, to keep boldly asking, to seek with an irresolvable, dogged desire and to knock with an unrelenting fervor. *Ask, and it will be given to you; seek, and you will find; knock, and it will be opened to you* (Matthew 7:7).

In the beginning, the Word (Christ awareness) was with God, and the Word (Christ) was God Himself, present and originally with God. The Word must be united with God consciousness in order for things to manifest into a real state of being. When the two (the Word and God) agree, it shall be established on earth.

> *Again I tell you, if two of you on earth agree* (harmonize together, make a symphony together) *about whatever* (anything and everything) *they may ask, it will come to pass and*

be done for them by My Father in heaven (Matthew 18:19).

When we first received salvation as babes in Christ, we began the transitional process of growing and maturing in Christ to become Sons and Daughters of God. We placed our faith in God. We imagined and believed that the Word of God is true. *Into Your hand I commit my spirit; You have redeemed me, O Lord God of truth* (Psalm 31:5).

Our conscious awareness of God's greatness grows when we realize He also created the answers to all of our prayers from before the foundation of the world. God consciousness increases the faith responses of our subconscious in the Spirit. Our enlightened imagination enables us to ascend into the realm of great faith where miracles are conceived, birthed and instantly manifested when our conscious aligns and unifies with the Holy Spirit to impregnate the subconscious.

The man in the following parable represents the virile consciousness of man:

> *When Jesus heard these things, He marveled at him,* (the masculine consciousness) *and turned around and said to the crowd that followed Him, "I say to you, I have not found such great faith, not even in Israel"* (Luke 7:9).

Another paradigm is observed in Matthew 15:28. The woman in this parable represents the fertile, receptive womb of the subconscious desire: *Then Jesus answered and said to her* (the feminine subconscious), *"O woman, great is your faith! Let it be to you as you desire." And her daughter was healed from that very hour.* For healing, deliverance or a miracle to occur, the sperm of God consciousness must impregnate the subconscious with the belief that nothing is impossible with God in order for great faith to be birthed.

Now having been taught mysteries by the Holy Spirit, the Spirit of Truth will develop the knowledge of our imagination, so we can gain the ability to utilize the faith of God. *Not boasting of things beyond measure, that is, in other men's labors, but having hope, that as your faith is increased, we shall be greatly enlarged by you in our sphere* (2 Corinthians 10:15). God promised to supply all of our requests, requirements and desires when we ascend into Christ's rich, imaginative realms created in glory. *And my God shall supply all your need according to His riches in glory by Christ Jesus* (Philippians 4:19).

Recognizing, receiving, resurrecting and resting in Jesus enables us to release the Christ within us. It is the understanding of the mystery of Christ dwelling within us that gives us the hope of reaching into the vast expanses of glory to obtain the promises of God that beckon us to come up higher in our knowledge of God. *To them God willed to make known what are the riches of the glory of this mystery among the Gentiles: which is Christ in you, the hope of glory* (Colossians 1:27).

The answers to our prayers have been standing in line, knocking and pressing at the doors of heaven. They have been waiting for us to enter into rest and thankfully petition God for their release. The answers to our prayers come to us from the very foundations of the world as we seek wisdom, knowledge, understanding and the face of Jesus by knocking on His glorious, eternal door. *Behold, I (Christ) stand at the door and knock. If anyone hears My voice and opens the door, I will come in to him and dine with him, and he with Me* (Revelation 3:20).

> *Revelation knowledge is used to both align and realign our imagination, so that wisdom can recalibrate our mind in order to redirect us onto a higher path.*

Jesus never gives up! He patiently stands at the door and waits for us to open up to Him. He never grows impatient or weary. He preservers. Jesus Christ is the eternal door on which we knock. Christ is also standing at and knocking on the door of our hearts.

Who will be the first one to open the door of their imagination, and let Him come in?

Our natural response to God's coming in to dine with us is one of praise, adoration, love and worship. Believers worship God in spirit and in truth. *All who dwell on the earth will worship Him, whose names have not been written in the Book of Life of the Lamb slain from the foundation of the world* (Revelation 13:8).

Jesus lovingly wrote the names of every person who will ever be conceived (even the millions prohibited from being born as a result of abortion) in the Lamb's Book of Life. He made the only way for all of mankind to be saved and experience eternal life. But at the fullness of time, the names of those who rejected His love, rebelled against His plan to save them and refused to receive Jesus' free gift of salvation will be blotted out of the Book of Life.

Revelation knowledge is used to both align and realign our imagination, so that wisdom can recalibrate our mind in order to redirect us onto a higher path. The knowledge we receive demands changes that transform, so that we can reach a higher spiritual order and dwell in a different mansion of existence. Revelation knowledge gives us the spiritual understanding necessary for us to speak peace to every storm of life. God created us in His image as a speaking spirit. We are to prayerfully speak, decree and prophesy the things He shows us. Our words frame an open doorway in order that the invisible can materialize and come out of the Spirit realm and into the natural realm.

Above the Storm

Peace and serenity reign
As unrest and disturbing winds
Roil the atmosphere below;
Stimulating new visions,
Representing potential life,
. . . choices.

Keat Wade 10/11/19 (12 Tishrei 5780)

Let your imagination run—while you peek through your portal window—as your plane carries you above the storm.

Because the authority we possess rests in God, the violent tempest has to obey us. The conflicts of life must dissipate and grow calm at the command of God's Word. When we catch the thief or destroyer, any damage the violent winds of the destructive hurricanes of life have caused must be repaid and restored sevenfold at a minimum. The level of restoration we experience is in direct proportion to the level of truth and spiritual understanding we presently walk in.

We are rewarded according to the measure of our faith. We can easily become the recipient of a thirty, sixty or hundredfold increase or repayment. With great faith, we can receive the abundant fullness of a thousandfold compensation. *May the Lord, the God of your fathers, make you a thousand times as many as you are and bless you as He has promised you* (Deuteronomy 1:11).

> *The imagination causes us to access the greatest levels of potential already within us that we have not yet tapped into.*

As we mature in God and learn how to actively trust and expectantly rest in His loving arms, we enter into the full measure of His abundance. God's blessings continue to overflow insuring that we continue to reach a level of spiritual return and physical recompense that flows above our heads with water, like Ezekiel's river, that is unable to be restrained.

> *Afterward he measured a thousand, and it was a river that I could not pass through, for the waters had raised, waters to swim in, a river that could not be passed over or through.*
>
> *And when these blessed waters shall enter into the putrid waters of the Dead Sea, the waters shall be healed and made fresh. And wherever this river of double blessings shall go, every living creature which swarms shall live. And there shall be a very great number of fish* (souls), *because these healing waters go to the Dead Sea waters that they may be healed and made fresh; and everything shall live wherever the river goes.*
>
> *All kinds of fruit trees will grow along the riverbanks. The leaves will never turn brown and fall, and there will always be fruit. There will be a new crop every month—without fail! For they are watered by the river flowing from the Temple. The fruit will be for food and the leaves for medicine to heal the nations* (Ezekiel 47:5, 8–9, 12).

God's grace dwelling within us gives us access to the endless measures of the river of faith. When we are faithful with the little that has been given to us, the Spirit of God will continue to increase by pouring out a greater measure of faith for us to grow in. We learn to navigate the depths of His rest as we swim in the wealth of His presence. This process will continue to challenge us throughout all of eternity.

> *And he pointed out to me a river of pure Water of Life, clear as crystal, flowing from the throne of God and the Lamb, coursing down the center of the main street. On each side of the river grew Trees of Life, bearing twelve crops of fruit, with a fresh crop each month; the leaves were used for medicine to heal the nations* (Revelation 22:1–2).

As Believers we will always be increasing, growing and flowing in the transformational River of Life, being changed into more of Christ's image and likeness.

This greater measure of faith empowers us to stand unshaken and persevere through tribulation in order to enter into the kingdom of heaven. When our faith is resting in the hope produced by God's glory, we can access the crystal clear, pure River of Life to enter into whatever heavenly dimension is needed. As we learn to submit to God, give Him thanks

Once our imagination is awakened, we can begin to relate to Christ as a creator.

for All Things and walk surrendered to His true wisdom, we learn how to maintain our right standing with Christ to receive our full inheritance.

The prophet Isaiah was incredibly bold when he said of God: *I was found by those who did not seek Me; I was made manifest to those who did not ask for Me* (Romans 10:20). Whatever state of being we react to and whatever philosophy, theory, person or being we believe in and accept as truth will dictate whether or not that thing or image will arise in us to manifest its power and presence.

But now made manifest, and by the prophetic Scriptures made known to all nations, according to the commandment of the everlasting God, for obedience to the faith (Romans 16:26). The greater the level of godly obedience we surrender to and we operate in, the more superior the measure of faith we can and will be trusted with.

The creative force found in God's revelation knowledge has been waiting for eternity for our imagination to discover it. God has concealed revelation knowledge for each of us to discover from before the foundation of the world. Revelation patiently waits for us in a predetermined state of existence. God's revelation has not been concealed from us but for us. Revelation longs to be imagined, seen, claimed, decreed and declared. Therefore, when different levels of revelation are believed and acted upon, the knowledge and power that is contained therein is manifested.

CHAPTER SEVEN

The Awakened Imagination

As we learned, the imagination dwells in the soul of man. It gives us the conscious power to move in the redemptive nature of God. Being born-again Believers, we are spiritually awakened to discern that Christ continually dwells within us. When Christ awakes in us, it stirs our imagination to see and recognize Him. Once our imagination is awakened, we can begin to relate to Christ as a Creator and the Lover of our soul. We then, in turn, become creative.

God's hidden truths are found in the beauty of Christ who is resting within our imagination. When we awaken to the splendor of Christ Who is within us, He will lift up our imagination to heavenly heights. We are clothed in Christ's love, grace and righteousness, so that we can take on and wear our godlike stature. To awaken and come forth as the new man in Christ, we should continually imagine ourself to be even better than we have ever imagined before. Greater is He that is in us than he that is in the world.

Let the greatness of Christ shine through you.

> *But when it pleased God, who separated me from my mother's womb and called me through His grace, to reveal His Son in me, that I might preach Him among the Gentiles, I did not immediately confer with flesh and blood (Galatians 1:15–16).*

Conferring with the natural, fleshly realms of carnal knowledge will keep us trapped in man's traditions that nullify the power of God working in our lives. But if we live by the Spirit of God within us, we will continue to grow and mature in spiritual knowledge, godly wisdom and truth so that we exercise in His love by demonstrating His truths..

The visionary form of sight is produced and governed by the imagination. The spiritual desire to obtain God's divine wisdom comes through acquiring a clear understanding of the revelation in God's Word that we have seen in a thought, dream or vision. Wisdom sees far beyond the natural by gazing into the vast expanses of the Spirit. When we embrace God's wisdom, His spiritual truths become our concrete reality.

The awakened imagination gives us the ability to see the truth about the treasury of the dormant gifts that are all currently at rest dwelling within. As each new gift is discovered, we learn to study how it functions in Christ. As we preserver in our spiritual training, we grow in skill and the power of His might. The imagination causes us to access the greatest

> *The power of the imagination is limitless; it enables us to explore the secrets of the universe.*

levels of potential already within us that we have not yet tapped into. Each of you must bring a gift in proportion to the way the Lord your God has blessed you (see Deuteronomy 16:17).

The imagination empowers us to reach our perfect, desired state, the way God sees us, and to confidently manifest the end results of our transformation. During this training, the imagination lets us explore the dramas of life's events over and over again until we get it right. We can watch the outcomes of various decisions to discern or learn which one will bring the highest route before we choose which happening to be actualized in our present life.

The imagination is the key to the endless doors of opportunity that lead into the boundless expanses of God. The power of the imagination is limitless; it enables us to explore the secrets of the universe. The imagination gives us glimpses of the future that exceed our current status, levels of knowledge, wisdom and understanding. Our wonderful, fantastic imagination is the doorway that empowers us to dream astonishing things. Our brilliant imagination endows us with the ability to know God, the One who shows us how to accomplish the impossible.

When we enter the heart of God, we gain the wisdom necessary to undertake the task of carrying out the impossible dream.

> *Then the King will turn to those on His right and say, "You have a special place in my Father's heart. Come and experience the full inheritance of the Kingdom realm that has been destined for you from before the foundation of the world"* (Matthew 25:34).

Our imaginative intellect that is physically joined with our obedient actions to the Word of God empowers us to multiply the knowledge of God. Our knowledge of God increases the Kingdom of Jesus in our own hearts. His divine power working within our spiritual imagination has given us All Things that pertain to life and godliness through the knowledge of Him who called us by His glory and virtue. We have been

Our awakened imagination is able to see these great promises God has for us..

given exceedingly great and precious promises that enable us to operate in God's peace. His grace empowers us to be partakers of the divine nature.

Our awakened imagination is able to see these great promises He has for us. Being able to believe God's promises empowers us to see the promises of God. Seeing His promises actualizes the power of love that is resident in them (for love covers a multitude of sin) to make it possible for us to take on the divine nature of God. The measure of God's love that is at work in our life determines the portion of exceeding greatness we will access, obtain and manifest. *By which have been given to us exceedingly great and precious promises, that through these you may be partakers of the divine nature, having escaped the corruption that is in the world through lust* (2 Peter 1:4).

God's omnipresence manifests in innumerable forms, yet He remains eternally the same. Every Believer can and will demonstrate God's divine nature in a different way by manifesting the works of Christ through their own unique personality. Believers extend God's wisdom, forgiving grace, love and transforming, healing miracle power to others. God does not diverge from His divine nature. Yet, in His vastness, He is always able to be Father, Brother, Savior and the Lover of our souls. God is always everything we need Him to be and eternally so much more.

Once we understand that greater is the Christ who is within us than he that is in the world, we can take on and mirror the characteristics and attributes of God's divine nature. His divine nature empowers us to act as His joint heirs and ambassadors to govern the world as His anointed Sons of God and demonstrates the IAMs of God. The Sons of God are conceived in holiness and led by faith in the Spirit of God. *For you are all Sons of God through faith in Christ Jesus. For all of you who were baptized into Christ have clothed yourselves with Christ* (Galatians 3:26).

As we continue to discover more about the Christ in us, we are emerging as the powerful Sons of God! Jesus is the God Man, the firstborn of many men and women who have taken on the powerful demonstration of His image and likeness.

Once the divine imagination of Christ is awakened within us, it diligently searches beyond our normal understanding to exceed the scope for God we currently hold. The imagination continually seeks further to know more of the Christ who is resident within us.

The creativity within our imagination reaches out to find the unexplored doors that will grant us the ability to expand to a thirty, sixty or hundred-fold measure of increase. When these levels are reached and mastered, we have been faithful with the little. We must continue to seek and war to enter into rest in order to go beyond the natural to reach a thousandfold increase, move into fullness, obtain God's abundance and then overflow into the dimension of multiplication that brings us into stewarding the dimensions of glory without measure.

We are to add faith to virtue and increase to knowledge in order to develop, obtain and sustain self-control. Then our continued perseverance will bring a multiplication of godliness and brotherly kindness, so that we always abound in the love and the knowledge of Christ (see 2 Peter 1:2–8; Matthew 13:23).

The voice of our imagination decrees: *May the Lord God of your fathers make you a thousand times more numerous than you are, and bless you as He has promised you* (Deuteronomy 1:11). When we agree with Christ's saving, transforming power, we experience addition, acceleration, increase and multiplication in the unlimited scope of the Spirit. *Again, I say to you that if two of you* (the conscious and the subconscious) *agree on earth concerning anything that they ask, it will be done for them by My Father in heaven* (Matthew 18:19).

We are well able to see, steward and continue to maintain the future vision of who we are destined to become in Christ. After a period of prayerful incubation and deliberate meditation on the Word, our actions change. Our inner faith talk becomes bold and more profound. We are able to both realize and fulfill our godly desires. What was once only an invitation to believe a vision becomes the fact of our future. *Therefore, I say to you, whatever things you ask when you pray, believe that you receive them, and you will have them* (Mark 11:24).

When our own subconscious agrees with our conscious desire in prayer, our spirit, soul and body (the triple cord that is not easily broken) come into unity. When the subconscious is in harmony with our conscious desire, they move in unison to join together as one. As the conscious and subconscious touch, knit together in one vision, joining in the power of unified agreement, the

> God has given the Believer the power to create and the wisdom to sustain that visionary mansion or attitude in order to alter his or her future state.

power created by the two becoming one causes the answers to our aspirational prayers to materialize.

The awakened imagination unifies the creative abilities found in the agreement of the conscious and subconscious desires, becoming one. Their harmony affords us the ability to walk in the strength of God's power. As we advance into God, we continually shed the old nature of sin, death and destruction. By taking on His image and likeness, the strength of our youth is renewed to war against our former spiritual ignorance and to free us to soar like the eagle to new heights of discovery. *As yet I am as strong this day as on the day that Moses sent me; just as my strength was then, so now is my strength for war, both for going out and for coming in* (Joshua 14:11).

The imaginative subconscious part of our mind is able to receive spiritual qualities and positive, life-giving attributes that empower us to stay young at heart and never grow old. It seems like it takes us a lifetime to develop into a quality person who is full of love, grace, mercy and kindness. It takes years to become someone who is patient and tolerant of others, one who has developed attributes of goodwill, peace and harmony by practicing brotherly love and self-sacrifice. When these spiritual qualities are resident, our spirit man remains soft, flexible and renewed in its youthful strength and appearance. The joy of the Lord truly is our strength. The faith of God transforms us into the image and likeness of God (see Genesis 1:26).

Humanity becomes what it focuses on or imagines. We maintain our present imaginative condition by continuing to believe God's truth and by taking positive, godly, peaceful actions. As we have learned, the logical mind of man cannot understand the truths of God. The natural man only sees a simple acorn in his hand. In contrast, the spiritual man sees expansive measure of the finished product: the majestic oak spreading its stately limbs to shade man and shelter God's creatures. If he continues to imagine, he will see, walk through and experience the emergence of a magnificent forest.

The strength and duration on which we can hold focused attention (the thing, state or goal imagined) determines the clarity of what our God consciousness can implant in the creative womb of our imagination.

> *Looking away from all that will distract to Jesus, who is the leader and the source of our faith giving the first incentive for our belief and is also its finisher bringing it to maturity and perfection. He, for the joy of obtaining the prize that was set before Him, endured the cross, despising and ignoring the shame, and is now seated at the right hand of the throne of God* (Hebrews 12:2).

All the events of our life must eventually come to pass by entering through the gate of the present in order to become a happening or reality in our world. When we imagine, see a divine vision, believe truth or take on the feelings of a future event (as if it has already occurred in our present life), we have possessed the clarity necessary to prophesy it into being. Our knowledge of Jesus dwelling within our imagination empowers us to perceive the image of the self in a very different, contrasted light. A specific example of seeing an altered state of ourselves can be drawn from Joel 3:10: *If we were weak before, we can now see and say that we are strong and becoming stronger still in the power of His might.*

The words that we hear, believe and say over ourself will create those active manifestations in our life. "Every day in every way, IAM growing stronger, wiser, and IAM prospering beyond my wildest imagination. IAM accepted in the Beloved, and people love me. IAM desirable and sought after. People offer me new opportunities that advance my realm of influence. IAM richly compensated for the wisdom, skills and expertise I possess."

This amazing practice of imagining and birthing something I have personally desired to be has happened for me many times. One of my first experiences was in junior high school. I always needed and sought help from one of my friends to pass my grammar classes. All the syntax, present and past perfect tenses and forms of "be or not to be" always kept me in confusion. None of it made any sense to me. One day, I desired to enter a writing contest. I told myself I would place well; I even fancied winning an award. I soon entered a writing contest. To my delight, I placed in the top five and won a $50 gift certificate.

> *A disciplined, focused imagination casts down every vain and wandering or negative image that tries to exalt itself against the knowledge of God's will for your life.*

Another similar recollection is when I attended Abraham Baldwin Agricultural College to receive my bachelor's degree in Animal Health Technology. I wanted to be a veterinarian, but I didn't pass the required calculus. So I settled for a two-year tech program instead. During my senior year, I needed to pass the Regents writing assessment in order to graduate. Although I was a straight A student and on the dean's list while carrying twenty hours a semester, the first time I took the test, I failed miserably. I had no idea how to write that type of structured paper. I knew if I wanted to pass the test, I would first need to overcome the fear of failure. Then I would need to change my thinking, I thought and believed I was a terrible writer. I would need to begin *seeing* (imagining) myself as a skilled writer.

I began with hiring a writing tutor and conferred with my brother Steven (Steven has always been a very skilled writer and excellent communicator). I practiced writing in a formal, structured manner. I visualized (imagined) myself being congratulated for passing the exam. I told myself I enjoyed writing and reminded myself of the skilled writers (like the late Governor Edward T. "Ned" Breathitt of Kentucky, a lawyer who wrote and passed Civil Rights legislative laws, and my late father Attorney Douglas H. Breathitt) in my family's bloodline. I *saw* myself writing an amazing essay that would enable me to pass the assessment. The second time I took the Regents, I passed with flying colors. Now twenty years later, I am what I saw and imagined myself to be. I love writing books and make my living as a published author of more than twenty books.

Faith in God grants the imagination the ability to access fresh revelation knowledge in the fourth dimension of the Spirit that is eager to gain access into our present, three-dimensional world or circumstances. When Believers see and imagine something that has been concealed for him or her in the invisible Spirit realm, he or she becomes the gateway that is able to reveal that particular mystery to humanity by utilizing the Spirit of Understanding.

God has given the Believer the power to create and the wisdom to sustain that visionary mansion or attitude in order to alter his or her future state. Praying from the realization of what has been believed and seen in the future causes faith to arise so that wisdom can materialize that desire in a now present state of existence.

> *Then I* (Wisdom) *was beside Him as a master craftsman; and I was daily His delight, rejoicing always before Him, rejoicing in His inhabited world* (the body of man), *and My delight was with the sons of men. Now therefore, listen to Me, My children, for blessed are those who keep My ways. Hear instruction and be wise and do not disdain it. Blessed is the man who listens to Me, watching daily at My gates, waiting at the posts of My doors. For whoever finds Me* (Wisdom) *finds life, and obtains favor from the Lord; but he who sins against Me*

(Wisdom) *wrongs his own soul; all those who hate Me* (Wisdom) *love death* (Proverbs 8:30–36).

Through practicing imaginative prayer that consistently places a demand on wisdom and the manifestation of the power of God's Word, and one's faith believing God, one can determine how to best walk out his or her own destiny.

Individuals can also decide to alter the prophetic vision of their future by choosing to manifest things in a higher realm by dwelling in a larger, more substantial mansion or existing in a state of great faith.

> *For Jews request a sign, and Greeks seek after wisdom; but we preach Christ crucified, to the Jews a stumbling block and to the Greeks foolishness, but to those who are called, both Jews and Greeks, Christ the power of God and the wisdom of God. Because the foolishness of God is wiser than men, and the weakness of God is stronger than men* (1 Corinthians 1:22–26).

To develop your visionary skills, try this activity:

> To relax, stimulate more creativity or experience a change of scenery, find a quiet, comfortable place. Close your eyes, take a few deep breaths, and then exhale all of your unwanted tension, and relax your body. Image your favorite peaceful place. See yourself walking on a beautiful, sunny beach with foamy waves gently washing over your bare feet. In a moment, you can travel to a peaceful, majestic mountaintop. Sit and rest on the cool iron bench that overlooks a deep carpet of brilliantly colored flowers covering the valley floor. Breathe in all of nature's clean fragrances that linger in the air after a spring rain. In this peaceful place of existence, ask God for His wisdom, clarity, or insightful answers to solve your every need. Continue to wait and focus on loving God until you see His provision or hear His Words of wisdom. Our imagination can take us anywhere in the world or into the worlds beyond in a moment of time.

Those who have awakened their imagination find they can travel wherever they focus their attention or desire without expending financial cost for their spiritual journey. Upon whatever they focus their imagination, seeing it manifested, hearing it and declaring its presence, they gain the needed understanding to advance into that very state of being. For them, they have already removed every excuse of why it is impossible or why it could not happen. fFor the person led by faith, the end resultit has already become their reality.

Thoughts create actions. Actions create habits. Good habits create a godly standard that develops a godly character that is full of integrity. Character formed and fashioned in God's image produces a grand destiny. When we focus our attention on conducting a certain godly image or creative imaginations, it begins to take on a clear form. The more we think about it, the more our lives begin to revolve around it. If we spend our time focused on loving, positive, life-giving thoughts, we will produce the light of God. On the other hand, if we dwell on dark, dismal, negative thoughts of anger, fear, failure, dread, hopelessness or despair, we will plummet into the depths of depression.

Imagery from On-High

Imagination that creates
Dread and fear is false thought,
Leading into a downward spiral
Of never ending emptiness.
Creative power comes through
Enlightened imagination,
Beamed down through divine
Throne room conduction.

Keat Wade 05/08/19 (3 Ayar 5779)

These anxious feelings are usually unfounded imaginary thoughts. Focusing on fear will always guide you onto the wrong path. Fear brings a paralysis that will cause you to fall captive to the chaos of failure. When they are resident in the mind, these toxic poisons produce, confusion, amnesia, dis-ease, unhealthy obsessions and abnormal complexes. We must stop focusing on problems and exhibiting self-defeating emotions; this will alleviate the feelings of dread and will prevent additional pain and catastrophic terror from weakening or possessing your soul.

Be careful not to emotionalize, empower or act out any negative thought. Instead instantly bind, renounce and cast down all fearful thoughts and actions. Do not retain the effects of evil. Never let them be internalized in the subconscious. Go to God in prayer, see His end plan, hear His comforting voice of direction, feel His loving arms of protection, glean from His wisdom, know that you have already obtained the answer and then walk it out. Your victory is assured.

> *God created our imagination with the capacity and capability to visualize and manifest anything we desire by focusing the attention of our faith upon it.*

The kingdom of heaven is within us. So, we can reach a place in God where we have access to all wisdom, all power and all knowledge, where all of our needs are supplied in the now realm of faith by His riches in glory. Jesus said:,

> *"We are to love the LORD our God with all the passionate thoughts and feeling that are within our heart, pray with all the emotional willpower that is within our soul, and with all the intelligence and creative capacity that is in our mind.' Love others as well as you love yourself for everything in God's law and the Prophets are contingent of getting these two things correct (Matthew 22:37–38).*

The Greek word 'mind' in this passage is *dianoia*, which means *imagination*. Jesus was saying that we must engage the creative power and illuminating abilities of our imagination in order to gain an enlarged capacity to love God and our neighbors in the proper way.

The subconscious mind responds or reacts as an active doer of the positive or negative suggestions it is fed. So relax, still your mind, let healthy thoughts from your conscious mind sink in in order to replace fear with faith and a bold, peaceful confidence that is a much higher thought process. Build up with nourishing, productive ideas of love to conquer and drive out fear. Come into harmony with the Word of God. Reflect on your goals. Let your inner images of hope arise giving wings to all the positive changes in your life. The death of fear is certain when you face it with the faith of God.

The thoughts we think and meditate upon release a sound or notable signal along with a corresponding radiant color of light. These colored lights and divergent sound signals send out an echoing beacon that attracts people who think similarly and hold identical views. Our subconscious houses past thoughts, memories and false beliefs, and our conscious houses our reasoning thoughts of the mind. These two areas of the mind will draw people to us

The imagination has the power to reshape, increase and prosper an existing future that has come into harmony with a God-given desire.

who mirror the equivalent actions, consistent beliefs and attitudes of the colored lights and sound frequencies we emit. These matching thought patterns of similar interests, characteristics, backgrounds and ideas is where the ancient proverb *birds of a feather flock together* come into play.

The imagination is responsible for drawing the team of friends and attracting the associates we need to assemble in order to obtain our goals and purposes to fulfill our calling and destiny. When we discover the immense power contained within the imagination, it would serve us well to spend quality time learning how to rule and rein over the thoughts and attitudes our imagination produces.

No matter what kind of injustice, abuse, neglect or theft you may have experienced at the hands of tyrannical mean-hearted people, no one has the power to control the thoughts of your mind or limit the creativity of your imagination. Once we realize it is the low frequency sounds and vibrations of our own adverse thoughts and despondent actions that have drawn destructive people and hurtful events into our life, we will be wise to repent and change the sound of our tune.

Lifting our voices in song—the giving of thanks, praise and worship—

revolutionizes the sound frequencies we are producing, so that God can inhabit us in a greater measure. When we are totally surrounded and immersed in God our conversation changes, everything is amended and our actions are modified for greatness to manifest.

Personal Reflection Moment

1. Take a moment to inventory your life. Ask yourself, "What is my imagination creating, projecting and drawing into my life?" It may seem like a simple question, but the answers may be extensive and require time to unfold.

2. Now invite Holy Spirit to help you process your answers. He will faithfully bring into light whatever needs to be amended. And if you seek His direction, He will give you all the wisdom, knowledge and revelation you need on how to proceed.

The awakened imagination has the God-given power to wipe out the works of darkness like sickness, disease, rebuke, depression and to remove the misery of poverty. It has the power to create in their place feelings and inspirational images that produce health, create wealth and gather to us the prosperity of God's abundant life.

Although the subject of prayer will be expanded on in Volumes II and III of the *IMAGINE* series, it is important to note here that the imagination must be coupled with the powerful force of prayer in order for the Spirit of God to alter or transform matters. Prayer changes individual people, collective cultural groups, societies and governments of the world. It is imperative to remember that every answer to prayer and anything we could ever desire, imagine or have need of has already been created and supplied by God during the Genesis of creation. It is our belief in God and the consistent exercise of the faith of God that motives the prayers we pray. When our spirit speaks in faith, confidently decrees God's Word and seeks His wisdom, the answers we need to empower us to create change are released to us.

The imagination has the power to visualize anything you focus your attention on. You must be careful to develop a focused control that concentrates your attention on one specific desire at a time. A disciplined, focused imagination casts down every vain and wandering or negative image that tries to exalt itself against the knowledge of God's will for your life. Take all poisonous thoughts captive. Replace them with a higher concept of self or a greater reality that you desire to achieve until that desired affect is consciously obtained.

> *Despite the fact that people knew the One True God, they did not glorify Him as God. Neither were they thankful for His goodness and provision. They have failed to show the love, honor, and appreciation due to the One who created them! Instead they have become futile and reprobate in their darkened thoughts and imaginations. Their lives are consumed by vain thoughts that poison their foolish hearts* (Romans 1:21).

God's angry displeasure erupts as acts of humanistic mistrust, socialism, communism, sexual wrongdoing and occult lying accumulate, as people try to put a shroud over God's truth. What's happening is this: People know God perfectly well, but when they don't treat Him like God, refusing to worship Him, they trivialize themselves into a destructive ignorance, silliness and confusion, so that there is neither any common sense nor godly wisdom left to direct their lives. They pretended to know it all, but they are base, void of knowledge and illiterate regarding life. They trade the glory of God, who holds the whole world in His hands, for cheap idols, and man's corrupt political agenda's, pushing for the one world order to arise with the antichrist as their god.

We are in a time just like it was at the Tower of Babel. Evil people organized around a cultic, humanistic agenda that worshipped self instead of God. They attempted to build a star tower that would allow them to ascend into the heavens as gods. They were one people, all of one mind or one world order. They all spoke the same language, believed the same lie and said the same thing.

> *GOD took one look at the vain imaginations of man's heart and said, "Will you look at that!" "One people, one language; why, this is only a first step, for the people are all together on*

this purpose. With one language they are able to imagine and start this kind of destructive project. This is only the beginning of what they will do. No telling what they'll come up with next—they'll stop at nothing! Soon they will think they can accomplish anything they purpose (or imagine) *to accomplish and everything in their own power. Come, we'll go down and garble their speech so they won't understand each other."*

Then GOD scattered them from there all over the world. And they had to quit building the city. That's how it came to be called Babel, because GOD confused and turned their language into "babble". From there God disbursed and scattered them all over the world (Genesis 11:6).

In the Hebrew language, the word 'purpose' is *yester*, and it means *imagination*. It is the same as the Greek word 'dianoia', which means *where people dwell together, unified in godly purposes, there the blessing of God is commanded.*

There is a spiritual law or principle that is activated when a people possess a oneness of mind, heart and soul. Unity of purpose or imagination causes people to see the same vision. A godly vision causes people to prosper, because it keeps them from perishing. People that come together and agree to accomplish one purpose will speak the same spiritual language and hold the same belief system, be it godly or ungodly.

> *Visions from our imagination are gateways that cause us to gain added insight and strategic, life-changing directions.*

The spiritual laws of God are truth, so they will work for the godly and the ungodly. Spiritual laws will cause God's blessing of rain to fall on the just and the unjust.

It is important to remain focused on the one thing until you learn to visualize its completion and feel it is being done. Agree that you already are that amazing person! Embrace all of the needed changes and start being and responding differently. Feel that ideal person emerging from within. Begin acting like that new person you envision by taking on that grand, new, Christlike identity. Manifest the reality of that remarkable, progressive person in your waking life. A wonderful image, fresh identity or inspirational idea is fueled or empowered by the degree you are able to focus your sustained attention and energy on fulfilling that incredible desire.

The degree of the power of God working within us can be measured by our ability to apply whatever things are true and noble, whatever things are just and pure, whatever things are lovely and of good report. If there is any virtue and if there is anything praiseworthy—meditate on these honorable things and shut down all negative thoughts, ideas or pursuits (see Philippians 4:8).

If our imagination is vain, double-minded, unstable, uncontrolled, fearful or unfocused, we will not see, sense or hear the Holy Spirit correctly; everything will be twisted or distorted. An unmotivated imagination will not feel or act in the right manner. Without a core, disciplined effort, we will not obtain the things that we desire regardless of how much energy we expend in prayer (see James 1:8).

> *When the prophets follow Jesus' example and prophesy as God commands them, God is able to manifest the greater works and creative miracles that will become commonplace.*

It is vital that we learn how to keep our inner imagination focused on Christ, on what He is doing and on how He is doing it. When we are centered on the right things, we will recreate a productive agreement between our beautiful, internal thought language and imagination and the outer manifestations of our world.

The emotional moods of our natural senses must submit their shifting tides of impressions to the higher function of the Holy Spirit moving through our spiritual senses. When we alter our conscious thoughts, it changes our subconscious mood. This changes the way our destiny is executed. Spiritual unity with Christ produces abundant blessings, prosperity and a higher life purpose.

God created our imagination with the capacity and capability to visualize and manifest anything we desire by focusing the attention of our faith upon it. Habitually thinking on things that are wholesome, honest, sensible, pure and are worth talking about bring forth the emotional and physical health and the spiritual wealth that opens our eyes to behold visions of prosperity.

> *I will bring the blind by a way they did not know; I will lead them in paths they have not known. I will make darkness light before them, and crooked places straight. These things I will do for them, and not forsake them* (Isaiah 42:16).

The wisdom that comes from God will straighten out any mess.

God never does anything part way. He completes to its utmost fullness whatever He begins. *Jesus said, If anyone loves Me, he will keep My Word; and My Father will love him, and We will come to him and make Our home with him* (John 14:23). God the Father, God the Son and God the Holy Spirit are all three living in their fullness within the heart of the Believer. Therefore, it is essential that we learn how to tap into the powers of the imagination in order to discover God in His fullness and the invisible world that surrounds us.

CHAPTER EIGHT

Imaginative Realms of Vision

Immeasurable opportunities and myriads of unlimited possibilities are at rest in the realms of the Spirit. God's imagination arises from the vast, creative depths found in the mind of Christ. Which one of us has been able to know the nature of Jesus in a manner that we can come into an understanding of the mind, counsels and purposes of the Lord? We have the mind of Christ, so that we can hold to the thoughts, feelings and purposes displayed in His heart (see 1 Corinthians 2:16).

The Spirit of Christ dwells within all of the past, present and future dimensions of eternity at the same time. We have the choice to dwell in any of these three realms at any time, but dwelling in the now, present realm of faith's reality is what prospers us the most. The mind of Christ lives and resides within the sanctified, objective imagination of the Believer. The imagination that is submitted to Christ can birth amazing, new possibilities. The imagination has the power to reshape, increase and prosper an existing future that has come into harmony with a God-given desire. However, without a heartfelt desire to learn, change or grow spiritually, we remain stationary, habitually motionless or sluggish, content to never reach our potential, thus falling short of the measure of the glory God intended for us to acquire. Starved of the desire for more, we do not lift a finger to advance, improve or embrace the struggle that is necessary to obtain the hope seen in the imaginative dreams of our future.

A God-given desire alerts us to our current need or condition. A spiritual yearning or longing compels us to take action. Believers should continually seek God for wisdom as He leads us in a new direction, so that we can gain a fresh vision in order to prosper.

Visions (imaginative thoughts) speak through the soft, inner voice of the spirit man. God communicates His desires to the natural man to show us how to take the proper actions to fulfill His will. When we are awakened spiritually and obediently follow the Spirit's voice, we gain the benefits of a vision.

When someone realizes that his or her vision is true, it has already become an assumed reality in his or her life (recalling the explanation of how the conscious and subconscious relate to one another will help solidify this concept). By accepting this truth, he or she gladly consents to the necessary changes that will cause his or her future to be rearranged, heightened, enlarged and manifested. This empowers it

The Spirit of Truth within our hearts empowers the imagination to show us what we are called to do and who we are destined to be.

to come into his or her present world. His or her conviction that the vision (dream) is a true reality confirms that his or her desired state has already been attained. To obtain what one has seen in a vision and to manifest it as a state of reality, one must be willing to think, feel and imagine what has been witnessed happening in the future as if it already has been experienced and recorded.

Visions carry an emotional impact that empowers our brain to record our visual images as an already happened event. Visions that are produced in our imagination become a treasured memory we can enjoy, revisit to study and relive in order to glean from it. Visions from our imagination are gateways that cause us to gain added insight and strategic, life-changing directions when it is needed. When our conscience accepts the end results of what we have already seen, we are able to take the right actions to bring that already-happened event into our present reality. When the conscience sees some things in vision form and believes it, what has only taken place in our imagination, it becomes fact to us. We are then able to adapt to those future facts by consciously mirroring their visionary images.

We must let go of the past and limited constructs in order to reconstruct a new framework to build something bigger and better. Changes in our imagination and our thoughts, beliefs and actions empower us to adjust to the modern reinvention of ourself. We can easily match up with or even surpass the higher vision of our future self. Believing is seeing!

> *We receive an upgraded, renewed mind of wisdom and an impartation of revelation knowledge from the Spirit of Truth.*

We learn to see things from the end results by maintaining our focused faith on becoming that end person or obtaining that end product. The desired transformation comes when we are able to see by faith, obtain by believing and consistently maintain our new identity. A new, Christlike image will empower us to reach our goals by transforming and disciplining our minds. When our spirit is strong, it will rule our body. A spiritual focus enables one to stay single-minded and determined to become the person who is able to do the will of God in his or her life.

The Apostle Paul prayed that the God of our Lord Jesus Christ, the Father of Glory, may give you the Spirit of Wisdom and revelation in the knowledge of Him (see Ephesians 1:15–17). The word 'revelation' in this powerful passage is the Greek prefix *epi* which means *super*. Paul was praying that Believers would have super revelation knowledge—*gnosis*.

> *[Paul prayed] that the eyes of our understanding would be enlightened, because he himself was enlightened by God's appearing to him in a blinding light on the road to Damascus. He prayed that each one of us would know the hope of His calling, the riches of the glory of His inheritance in the saints, and the exceeding greatness of His power toward us who believe, according to the working of His mighty power which He worked in Christ when He raised Him from the dead and seated Him at His right hand in heavenly places, far above all principalities and powers, might and dominion, and every name that is*

named, not only in this age but also in the era that is to come.
And He put All Things under His feet, and gave Him to be
head over All Things to the church, which is His unified body,
the fullness of Him who fills all in all (Ephesians 1:18–23).

The unified body of Believers, the Church of Jesus Christ are the manifested fullness of God on the earth.

We are transformed into the Kingdom of God when we, like innocent children, trust and believe in the inventive, revelatory power of God's Word. We are changed when we practice growing up into the wisdom found in the power of His creative, foundational truth. God's truth continually transforms us by the renewing of our minds, so that the Spirit of the mind of Christ is constantly emerging and working

> *God's counsel and wisdom come to reposition us, so that we can gain more understanding of how to operate and prosper in another realm of glory.*

in and through us (see Ephesians 1:19-21). The renewed mind of Christ dwelling within our heart causes us to be flexible. The more we change into the likeness and image of God, the more our future is altered, improved, increased and expanded.

God has prepared detailed future plans for each and every one of us to sequentially advance and prosper beyond our wildest dreams. *As it is written: "Eye has not seen, nor ear heard, nor have entered into the heart of man the things which God has prepared for those who love Him"* (1 Corinthians 2:9).

The God-given choice to change or to remain the same is always ours.

Personal Reflection Moment

1. Which future will you choose?

2. Will you choose God's highest plan for your destiny? Are you willing to be transformed for God's goodness and mercy to follow you all the days of your life?

Dr. Barbie L. Breathitt

3. Will you gladly make the sacrifices necessary to obtain all the highest and best that God has lovingly reserved for you? Or when opportunity knocks, will you settle for the easy way out and choose the low, broad road of mediocrity that leads to destruction?

The love of God takes up His residence within the heart of man and continually transforms. He inspires us to take on His image. The Holy Spirit's eternal presence sustains us in all that we do. God will never leave or forsake us. His presence is always resting within every Believer. The measure of faith we possess determines the amount of Christ's recognizable presence moving within us. The degree that our spiritual understanding has ascended into the realms of glory determines the portion of God's power measured out to us to begin its work within us.

> *While we do not look at the things which are seen, but at the things which are not seen. For the things which are seen* (earthly) *are temporary, but the things which are not seen* (spiritual imagination) *are eternal* (2 Corinthians 4:18).

Paul announced to the Believer that by faith God calls those (invisible, spiritual things that exist in the imagination) things which do not exist as though they did (see Romans 4:17).

We see things by faith that are invisible, then we learn how to operate in spiritually perceived spiritual truths to frame our world by God's creative Word (see Hebrews 11:3).

My inner beliefs, found in the fertile loins of the imaginations of my mind, mediate my potential to reach my destiny. My personal beliefs reveal my true emotional attitudes, precepts and the conceptions I hold true of myself, of others and of God.

> *But All Things become visible when they are exposed to the light of God's precepts, for it is God's light that makes everything visible. For this reason, He says, "Awake, sleeper and arise from the dead, and Christ will shine as a new day dawning upon you and give you light"* (Ephesians 5:13–14).

Our faith has the ability to reach into the future and draw out what is needed into our present *now* situation. We believe it, see it and pray God's perfect will. We speak the Word of God until the imagination pictures it as an already happened event. Bringing the future increase into our *now* produces spiritual acceleration. Another name for it is a miracle.

Miracles accelerate and speed up nature's timetable by altering or quickening the natural sequence of events that were already planned. In order to manifest something different than our current situation or level of understanding, we must prophesy what the Word of God commands in first person, present tense. By believing, seeing, declaring and decreeing the Word of God in the *now* realm of faith, we stop delaying what we hope to attain.

God wants His prophets to begin to exaggerate His greatness. God wants us to magnify Him with the words of our mouth. We need to build an entry point and grand platform that is big enough to host God's awesome presence. When prophets prophesy that God will come to do something in the future, God's coming is postponed until some distant time. God's coming is delayed. Instead of God being able to insert Himself into the situation to perform a miracle now, He has to wait until the specific time period that was announced in order to honor the word of the prophet.

Some prophets may operate in this manner because they question whether God will actually *show up* if they were to boldly declare a thing that is not as if it were. To save face, they prophesy that God will manifest His presence in a certain time period instead of allowing Him to burst onto the scene *now*! Jesus made Himself of no reputation. He only said and did what He saw and heard His Father doing in the now. When the prophets follow Jesus' example and prophesy as God commands them, God is able to manifest the greater works and creative miracles that will become commonplace as the Sons of God arise as One New Man.

The creative energy force of faith is NOW! Faith invades the present moment and prompts us to ask, decree and believe to see the impossible. Faith is not productive if it is reserved for some far-off future event. *You have commanded us to keep Your precepts diligently* (Psalm 119:4). When we learn to magnify the Lord, trusting that God is the Almighty, we will boldly exaggerate and demonstrate the goodness of God.

Dr. Barbie L. Breathitt

When Believers magnify the Lord, they give Him a larger platform of expression from which He can demonstrate His unlimited, creative, miracle power. Great faith does not judge after appearances. Creative faith shuts the access door to negative thoughts, feelings or facts. *I will meditate on Your precepts, and contemplate Your ways* (Psalm 119:15).

We must be conscious of taking on the spiritual function of a thing hoped for in order for us to become or apprehend that thing. We have to embrace the transformational power of faith to become what we are prophesying and seeking. *Behold, I long for Your precepts; revive me in Your righteousness* (Psalm 119:40).

Shutting the door to the natural realm and focusing on being in the Spirit of God, His presence brings us into a place of liberty. *And I will walk at liberty, for I seek Your precepts* (Psalm 119:45). As we maintain the presence of God's liberty as our focus (seeking the Kingdom of God first), all of these other things are added unto us. *This has become mine, because I kept Your precepts* (Psalm 119:56).

When we are not conscious of the Lord's presence residing within us, we often think, "I hope I will be able to obtain my objective. I hope I will receive an answer to prayer sometime in the future. I hope God will heal, save or deliver me." Our life goal is to be like Jesus in our declarations and actions. *The works of His hands are truth and justice; all of His precepts are sure* (Psalm 111:7).

Believers who have been enlightened by the Spirit of God fervently seek the favor of Christ's face by considering all His ways as just and right. *Make me understand the way of Your precepts; so, shall I meditate on Your wonderful works* (Psalm 119:27). When the Lord Jesus is in His holy temple (our body), He is the IAM of all. Jesus is the first and the last. He is the God who is above all, in all and through all. Jesus Christ is the IAM that IAM (past, present, future and forevermore) eternally dwelling within our consciousness.

True Believers keep God's vision continually before their mind's eye, in the heart of their imagination. *No one can come to Me unless the Father who sent Me draws him; and I will raise him up at the last day* (John 6:44). The mysteries of Christ's gospel of grace, of us being co-heirs to His promises through becoming one with Him, have been held secret in previous generations. *But the mysteries of Christ have now been revealed to Believers through the understanding that the Holy Spirit gave to His sacred prophets and apostles* (Ephesians 3:3–6).

CHAPTER NINE

Spiritual Truth and Divine Wisdom

To know the Person of Truth and to become a person of truth, we must have the Spirit of Truth living within us, directing the thoughts of our imagination, expectations and actions as one unified front. *The world cannot receive the Spirit of Truth because it neither sees God, nor knows Him; but the Believer knows Him, for Truth dwells with us as Emanuel and is also within us as the Holy Spirit* (John 14:17).

The Spirit of Truth comes to us to reveal Jesus; He is the reality of truth. Christ is the Spirit of Truth that has been placed within each Believer. He will prophetically lead and guide us into all truth, both internally and externally, by revealing Himself to us in this present world and in the next. *The Spirit of Truth will not speak His own message; but He will only announce what He hears from His Father, and He will tell us the future and show us what is yet to come* (John 16:13).

Staying True

Reject the questioning voices,
Spoken forth as truth,
From the mouths of,
Those who know not truth.
They speak out of vain imagination,
Not grasping understanding of the,
Source of their evil thoughts,
Intended to dishonor our God.
Listen closely to gain Holy Spirit,
Understanding of God-centered truth,
From on high, ringing out,
Echoing from heavenly chambers,
. . . "Hear the voice of I AM!"

Keat Wade 05/09/19 (4 Iyar 5779)

Truth is embodied in a spiritual personage of Christ. Jesus contains the fidelity of the original standard of the real thing. Truth is a sincere action, character or event. Truth is defined as the transcendent fundamental or spiritual reality, an accurate judgment or insightful proposition. Truth is the utterance of an idea that is certain or accepted as true; the property of the statement is in one accord with the reality of the actual facts.

Real truth cannot exist individually or according to what each person perceives as his or her personal reality of truth. Truth must hold to the highest standard of God, the Spirit of Truth. Tangible truth is only found in God! Life-changing, transformational truth is found demonstrated in the power of the Word. Reality is found in the life-saving, healing and delivering gospel truth of Jesus Christ. Our truth depends on the measurement of belief we have in the Spirit of Truth (Jesus) who dwells within us.

People imitate on whatever they focus or with whomever they spend their time. The bible warns, *Do not be deceived: Evil company corrupts good habits* (1 Corinthians 15:33). In the same regard, the opposite is also true.

Good company forms incorruptible, good habits within us. Discovering and communing with the Christ within us provokes our imagination to think on higher, pure, lovely and holy things. *As a man thinks in his heart (imagination), so is he* (Proverbs 23:7).

The heart (imagination) either acts like the natural man who does not embrace the things of the Spirit of God, because they are foolish to him. Or the heart perceives the wisdom and power of divine, spiritual things and lives far beyond all limitations in a four-dimensional world where all possibilities are now realities.

> *God's truth will carefully lead us into the depths of the Spirit and continually guide us into the highest possible connection as we journey through life.*

We are either the Samaritan woman at the well drawing buckets of water, or we are Jesus bringing eternal, living water. We are the crippled man at the pool waiting for someone to put him in the healing water, or we are the man who cries out to Jesus and then takes up his own mat to walk and leap. We are either the nine lepers who were healed but didn't return to give thanks, or we are the one lone leper who was both healed and made completely whole (entered into the power of multiplication) when he returned to thank Jesus.

The Legion of Demons Behind the Riotous Destructive Mob

As Jesus exited the boat on the shore of the Gadarenes, immediately He was met by a naked madman totally possessed by a mob of unclean spirits. He could no longer think for himself but could only do what the demons compelled him to do. He existed among the tombs and graves of the cemetery. Because of the demon power within him, no one person, police or military could tame, bind, restrain or hold him with ropes, not even with shackles and chains. Night and day he spewed his lying propaganda, cried out filth and curses from his tormented, twisted mind and cut and slashed himself with sharp objects and stones. He wandered the dark streets scaring people, murdering and destroying property. Then he would retreat to his home in the mountain graves and tombs.

When he first saw Jesus a long way off, the real man within had a spark of hope for freedom from his bondage to evil. So, he ran and bowed down to worship Him. The compassion in Jesus commanded the evil spirits, "Get out and leave the man!" But immediately, the demons within the man cried out in an animalistic roar that bellowed with a loud voice in protest, "I have rights! My life matters! I can do whatever I want, kill, steal and destroy, and no one can stop me! What business do I have with You, Jesus, Son of the Most High God? I implore You by God that You do not torment, mess with me or give me a hard time." Jesus asked the evil spirit's name. They replied, "My name is riotous, lawless mob of prejudice, hated, murder and destruction; for we are a legion of many, anarchist and evildo-ers controlled by the antichrist spirit." Then in desperation, the riotous mob of insurrectionist spirits begged Jesus not to banish them from the country. Thousands of unclean demons of dev-astation pleaded with Jesus, "If you bind and cast us out of this young man, please cast us into the herd of filthy pigs so we can live in the swine's bodies." Jesus commanded them to leave the youth's body. When the mob of riotous demons entered the pigs, the swine went mad. Crazed with insanity, irrational mental illness, absurd recklessness and crazed stupidity, the whole herd stampeded off the cliff and drowned in the sea.

Those who tended the pigs ran to tell the towns and whole country what had happened to the riotous mob of demons that had possessed the young man. Everyone wanted to see and know what had happened to the legion of evil spirits that had haunted the tomb of the madman's mind. When they came to Jesus, they saw the previously crazed, insane madman, dressed in clothes, delivered from his prejudice and hate and at peace into his right mind, sitting quietly while listening to Jesus (see Mark 5:1–15).

Because I am what I think, if the thoughts of my heart are of hurt, lack, jealousy or anything other unlovely, I will reside in a limited mental state of existence. However, if I clothe myself in God's Word and eternal truth, continually feasting my thoughts upon their life-giving, creative power, I will immediately ascend. My new beliefs produce a higher view that releases a feeling of freedom. When the Spirit liberates me, I break out of my previous, lowly frame of reference. A higher realm of truth empowers me to ascend into a higher state of becoming and being. I become what I focus on and feast upon. There have been numerous instances in my life where I have needed to shift from functioning out of my own truth (thoughts) to operating in God's truth.

> *"For my thoughts are not your thoughts, neither are your ways my ways," declares the Lord. "As the heavens are higher than the earth, so are My ways higher than your ways and My thoughts than your thoughts"* (Isaiah 55:8–9).

Based on past experiences, I used to expect to be rejected in relationships after a certain amount of time. So when that time period would roll around, I started looking for rejection and anticipating the pain that comes with that type of harsh dismissal. We get what we expect, focus on, predict and await. It becomes a self-fulfilling prophecy.

When I finally realized I was inviting rejection and drawing it to myself with my negative thoughts, actions and faith, I repented. I stopped expecting to be rejected. I decided to change my focus from foreseeing rejection that destroyed relationships to developing the idea that I was sought after, desired, wanted and accepted. Once I was accepted, I changed my focus to being celebrated. Once I was celebrated, I changed my focus to being cherished. I soon discovered that when I saw myself in any positive manner, I could draw those types of affirmative, constructive, encouraging people to myself who accepted, celebrated and cherished me. Amazing, upbeat, confident people came streaming into my life. I learned I could become whoever I saw myself becoming. I could draw to myself whatever I wanted.

No one wants to be rejected or dismissed. Everyone wants to be accepted and cherished. It is our decision to believe the truth that God says about us. God says we are accepted in the Beloved; we are fearfully and wonderfully made in His image. We all have the potential to reflect God's beauty, but we must choose to develop ourselves into His likeness. When we put on His robes of righteousness, kindness, goodness, mercy or any other of His godly characteristics, we wear the royal garments from His closet as our own. When we are covered with His attributes, it is hard to discern where the light of our shining stops, and His glory cloud begins.

As we clothe ourselves with the cloud of Jesus' truth, we no longer move in time. Instead, we learn how to travel in His eternal truth. Those who refuse to use their imagination have no wind under their wings to give them a lift in life. When I meditate on the Spirit of Truth being in and with me as Emanuel, the pillar of fire is illuminated in my mind's eye. The brilliant fire lights my path, my way, my truth, and it becomes my imagination's guiding light.

> *Those who willingly lose their lives in order to serve God's purposes on earth, indeed, receive untold promises and glorious rewards.*

The Way, the Truth and the Life are the triple cords by which we live and strengthen our lives in this world. The Spirit of Truth builds a platform of character, honesty and integrity within us. Some people continually look for a sign or a miracle, while others seek solely after wisdom. But mature Believers seek after eternal truth in knowing the person of Christ. Believers long to know Him who was crucified on the cross for the healing of their sin and disease and is now resurrected in the power and wisdom of God living within them (see 1 Corinthians 1:22–25).

When our minds are fully persuaded that the Christ within us is both the author and finisher of our faith, we prophesy what He discloses from the center stage of righteous, visionary sight. We agree with God's grand plan. *He also established them forever and ever; He made a decree which shall not pass away. He fixed their bounds which cannot be passed over* (Psalm 148:6). We believe, imagine and then decree the future from the realm of eternity on a platform of right standing that sees the truth of God's perfect, future will. *I will declare the decree of the Lord: He said to Me, You are My Son; this day I declare I have begotten You* (Psalm 2:7).

The truth of God first implants a vision of one's true self into his or her imagination. *O send out Your light and Your truth, let them lead me; let them bring me to Your holy hill and to Your dwelling* (Psalm 43:3). Then the truth of the Word found in the declarative words of prophecy, outline the step-by-step plans for taking on the image of what was shown in the private viewing chambers of the heart. *Guide me in Your truth and faithfulness and teach me, for You are the God of my salvation; for You, only You do I expectantly wait all the day long* (Psalm 25:5).

The Spirit of Truth within our hearts empowers the imagination to show us what we are called to do and who we are destined to be. *Now therefore, if you will obey My voice in truth and keep My covenant, then you shall be My own peculiar possession and treasure from among and above all peoples; for all the earth is Mine* (Exodus 19:5).

This inner light of revelation knowledge gives us the prototype that transforms our inner being. *His lamp shone above and upon my head and by His light, I walked through darkness* (Job 29:3). As we awaken to take on this new image of light, making the necessary alterations, our inner transformation slowly trickles into our outer world. *To them God willed to make known what are the riches of the glory of this mystery among the Gentiles: which is Christ in you, the hope of glory* (Colossians 1:27).

> *By allowing God's guiding light to luminously blaze from within us, we draw those in darkness unto Christ.*

The voice of Christ's presence residing within us creates godly concepts that establish a platform for the existence of His glory to manifest within us. When we agree with the creative, transforming power of our imagination, we become one with that image.

> *Two are better than one* (Christ and you), *because they have a good reward for their labor. For if they fall, one* (Christ) *will lift up his companion* (you). *But woe to him who is alone* (unsaved) *when he falls for he has no one to help him up. Again, if two* (Christ and you) *lie down together, they will keep warm; but how can one* (the unsaved) *be warm alone? Though one* (you) *may be overpowered by another, two* (Christ and you) *can withstand him. And a threefold cord* (God the Father, Jesus Christ the Son and the Holy Spirit) *is not quickly broken* (Ecclesiastes 4:9–12).

The presence of Christ Jesus, the Father and the Holy Spirit residing within us as the threefold Trinity is the unbreakable combination of supreme strength, divine wisdom and visionary power. If God is for you, who can be against you or defeat you?

> *Examine yourselves as to whether you are in the faith. Test yourselves. Do you not know yourselves that Jesus Christ is in you?—Unless indeed you are disqualified. But I trust that you will know that we are not disqualified* (2 Corinthians 13:5–6).

We receive an upgraded, renewed mind of wisdom and an impartation of revelation knowledge from the Spirit of Truth. In order for us to ascend to a new level and dwell in this higher dimension of the Spirit, our present beliefs must change. God's grace empowers us to find the answers to life that are contained in chambers of divine intelligence and wisdom. When we consciously believe spiritual truths and our faith agrees with this heavenly union, our thoughts are changed from a natural sphere into a loftier way of thinking. The higher thoughts of our mind become one with the mind of Christ.

The spirit of a person is the only one who knows the hidden impulses, reactions and responses of that particular person. It is the same with God. The Holy Spirit is the only One who fully understands the secret thoughts and actions of the Spirit of God (see 1 Corinthians 2:11). This encounter with the Spirit of Wisdom (who grants us the power to consciously recognize the integral presence of God) becomes part of our DNA. Having lived it, we can recall the experience as an already happened event or memory. Now that we have entered into a transformed state, we can consistently relate to worldly affairs from being seated in this higher and heavenly state of being.

God's illuminating light within us—His presence—allows us to enter into rest.

The Bible states wisdom is not of this world. The manifestation of our objective world is always a reflection of our inner, subconscious thoughts and beliefs.

Dr. Barbie L. Breathitt

So, where does wisdom come from? And where does insight live? It can't be found by looking, no matter how deep we dig, no matter how high we fly. If we search through the graveyard and question the dead, they say, "We've only heard rumors of it." God alone knows the way to wisdom. He knows the exact place to find it. God knows where everything is located within us, in heaven, and on and under the earth. God controls the vast expanses of the heavens for it has endless layers. God created, sustains, sees and knows everything under the heavens. After God commanded the winds to blow and measured out the waters, He arranged for the rain and set off explosions of thunder and lightning. God focused on wisdom, made sure it was all set and tested and ready. Then He addressed the human race: "Here it is! The Fear of the Lord—that's wisdom, and insightful understanding means the shunning of evil" (Job 28:20–28).

The great wisdom of the ages begins when man learns to reverently fear God. The wicked have clouded their understanding which leads them into foolishness, snares and death. Job walked in godly wisdom and is known for the wisdom he gained through his intimate relationship with God.

Job continued. "Ah, that I were as I once was, months ago during the time when God oversaw me, when His lamp of truth shone above my head, and by His light, I walked through the darkness. Ah, to be in the ripest time of life once more— when the intimacies of friendship with God enfolded my tent, when the Highest One was with me and my children encircled me, when my steps were bathed in milk and the rock poured out rivers of olive oil, showering my body, when I went up to the gate of the city, when I took my seat in the town square where the elders meet. There the young saw me and they made room for me, in deference to the other elders. The old rose and stood out of respect. The leaders stopped talking with their hands over their mouths. The voices of nobles fell to a hush; their tongues stuck to the roofs of their mouths. Every ear that heard me blessed me, and every eye that saw me testified to my greatness. After all, I rescued the poor when they cried out for help and assisted the orphans when they had no one else. The dying spoke their blessings over me, and the widows sang their joyful songs honoring what I did. I adorned myself in righteousness, and it covered me; my justice fit me like a cloak and turban—conveying both my dignity and my authority. I was the eye for the blind, the feet for the lame, a father for the needy, and I sought for the cause of whom I did not know. I broke out the fangs of the wicked and wrested prey from their jaws.

Then I said, 'I will pass from this earth in the comfort of my nest. My days will be more numerous than a beach's grains of sand. My roots will grow deep, spreading out to the water's edge, and in the night, the dew will come to rest on my branches. Respect will be accorded me every day, my skill with the bow always new in my hand.'

People used to listen to me, the sense of expectation visible on their faces; they waited in silence for my advice. And when I finished, they did not hurry to speak again. They waited while my words dropped like dew upon them. Indeed, they waited for me as one waits for a good rain, and they opened their mouths as if to catch spring showers on their tongues. I smiled upon them when their confidence flagged, and they took comfort in my beaming face. I led them in their way. I sat as their leader. I lived like a king among his troops. I was as a happy man spreading comfort among the mourners" (Job 29:1–25).

God gives us the needed wisdom. He is our eternal resource for everything we need. *Where there is no revelation, the people cast off restraint; but blessed is the one who heeds wisdom's instruction* (Proverbs 29:18). Because God's wisdom is not found in this world, it is only obtained when we are willing to transition from one level of the anointing to a higher realm of glory and then to another and another. The obtainment of wisdom requires a disciplined spiritual motion and advancement. Our spirit grows when we are able to move past the anointing to attain a fresh, new realm of glory.

We ascend when we repent, change our attitude and behavior or open our mind to agree with a more complex truth. God's counsel and wisdom come to reposition us, so that we can gain more understanding of how to operate and prosper in another realm of glory. If we continue to do the same thing in the same way, we will always get the same results.

> *But where can wisdom be found? And where is the place of understanding? Man does not know its value, nor is it found in the land of the living. From where then does wisdom come? And where is the place of understanding? It is hidden from the eyes of all living, and concealed from the birds of the air. Destruction and Death say, "We have heard a report about it with our ears. God understands its way, and He knows its place."*

> *When God questioned Job, he answered the Lord and said: "I know that You can do everything, and that no purpose of Yours can be withheld from You. You asked, 'Who is this who hides counsel without knowledge?' Therefore, I have uttered what I did not understand, things too wonderful for me, which I did not know. Listen, please, and let me speak; You said, 'I will question you, and you shall answer Me.' I have heard of You by the hearing of the ear* (by what has been told to me by others or man's traditions), *but now my own eye sees You. Therefore, I abhor myself, and repent in dust and ashes"* (Job 28:12–13, 20–23).

When we gaze at life through our natural eyes, we can be deceived to blindly believe a lie. But if we focus our vision based on the clarity of our spiritual eyes, we will always see God's truth and His mighty hands boldly reigning in our lives. Paul was sincere when he wrote, *For our boasting is this: the testimony of our conscience that we conducted ourselves in the world in simplicity and godly sincerity, not with fleshly wisdom but by the grace of God, and more abundantly toward you* (2 Corinthians 1:12).

When a Believer recognizes something in his or her life that needs to be repented of (put to death and then transformed into a higher order and resurrected into the power of the new life found in Christ), he or she defeats the enemies of resistance who dwell within and makes room for him or her to take on more of the image of Christ.

Wisdom cries out excellent things for people to gain a heart of discretion and godly understanding and to know how to walk on the path of a prudent life. The mouth of wisdom speaks righteousness and truth to reveal godly knowledge and instruction that is better than silver, gold and the finest of rubies. Wisdom hates the evil pride and arrogance of a perverse mouth. Wisdom brings sound, wise counsel, understanding and strength for kings, princes and nobles to reign, rule and judge justly.

Wisdom loves and rewards those who love and diligently seek after her. As we walk in righteousness and honor God, wisdom grants us the ability to inherit wealth with enduring riches to fill our treasuries. Wisdom is the master craftsman who delights and rejoices over the sons of men inhabiting the world. Wisdom blesses those who keep her ways, intently listen, carefully watch and wait for her wise, divine instructions. Whoever finds wisdom finds life and obtains favor from the Lord. But whoever sins against or hates wisdom wrongs his own soul and loves death (see Proverbs 8).

Entering into rest is to enter into God's presence.

The still, small voice of God echoes His desires within the chambers of the Believer's heart. When His Words are written upon the tablets of the Believer's heart, his or her life becomes God's living message. The voice of the Holy Spirit trains our inner voice to resonate on the identical, beautiful frequency of heaven. When we tune our ears to hear Christ's creative speech within us, we will say what we hear Him saying. Christ's Words of wisdom create a new, visionary world of open doors and vast, unlimited opportunities filled with heavenly knowledge. Listen to that little voice in your heart that says, "I wish we could!" Then agree to try your best, and say, "Yes, we can!" The love language of the imagination is the freedom to see and to be anything you desire.

When we agree with the internal Spirit of Christ, the mental dialogues we hold within our being become a declaration of praise we raise as a shout from the rooftops. The victories and the positive or negative outcomes we experience are presently manifesting in our life due to the voice of our inner speech, self-concepts and belief systems.

The way we see ourself, who we truly are and who we believe the Spirit of Christ is within us, determines the world that surrounds us. If we feel we are well able and capable of arising to any occasion, we will draw on the Christ in us to gain the wisdom, knowledge and strength needed to accomplish any feat. God's visions allow us to see ourself doing the will of our Father.

> *Who is wise and understanding among you? Let him show by good conduct that his works are done in the meekness of wisdom. But if you have bitter envy and self-seeking in your hearts, do not boast and lie against the truth. This wisdom does not descend from above, but is earthly, sensual, and demonically inspired. For where envy and self-seeking exist, confusion and every evil thing abide. To those who are defiled and unbelieving nothing is pure; but even their mind and conscience are defiled* (Titus 1:15).

God's truth will carefully lead us into the depths of the Spirit and continually guide us into the highest possible connection as we journey through life. *But the wisdom that is from above is first pure, then peaceable, gentle, willing to yield, full of mercy and good fruits, without partiality and without hypocrisy* (James 3:17).

In contrast, those who do not believe they are capable, qualified and intelligent or strong enough will fail; they will fulfill their own negative prophecy. That which we do not claim as true for ourself will never be realized by us. *For whoever has, to him more will be given, and he will have abundance; but whoever does not have, even what he has will be taken away from him* (Matthew 13:12).

We acquire the promises of God through patiently resting in His presence.

This God-given principle of creation works through our senses of seeing, hearing, saying and believing. Our imagination carries us into the future to see the vast possibilities available for us to own and occupy. But if we do not believe we are able to secure them for ourself, they will never become our reality.

And after you have suffered a little while, the God of all grace

> *Who imparts all blessing and favor, Who has called you to His own eternal glory in Christ Jesus, will Himself complete and make you what you ought to be, establish and ground you securely, and strengthen, and settle you* (1 Peter 5:10).

When Jesus appears (and we are conscious of seeing Him), our imagination is awakened. We are instantly transformed into His image. *As for me, I will see Your face in righteousness; I shall be satisfied when I awake in Your likeness* (Psalm 17:15).

When the imagination becomes awakened, it becomes the Merkabah Chariot of God, the spiritual transportation device upon which Jesus is able to come and appear to us again and again. *But who can endure the day of His coming? And who can stand when He appears? For He is like a refiner's fire or a launderer's soap* (Malachi 3:2).

CHAPTER TEN

The Guiding Light

God's omnipresence surpasses the farthest reaches of the universe. God has prepared an eternal kingdom designed to dwell within the heart of man. Before God created and stretched out the heavens, He skillfully formed the earth and all the creatures that inhabit the land, sky and seas. God did not create anything in vain; He made the whole world to be populated and covered with His ever-expanding glory.

God brought forth the principle of the seed-bearing plants and vegetation. And He established everything else that comes from the earth with the ability to reproduce after its kind.

> *I assure you and most solemnly say to you, unless a grain of wheat falls into the earth and dies, it abides by itself alone, just one grain, never more. But if it dies, it bears and produces much fruit for a bountiful harvest in every area of life* (John 12:24).

God gave mankind His creative breath (His life-giving Spirit and consciousness) to all who live upon the earth. God thought, imagined, envisioned and planned everything. God's dream drew up the destiny blueprints for all of creation. The Trinity imagined the perfect world where He and man could walk, talk and dwell together, unified as One New Man in the Spirit. God formed the first man out of the dust of the earth. The three-in-one

God created man in His own image and likeness.

The imaginative mind (Ruach, creative breath or will of God's Spirit) then spoke the words that quickened man's soul and allowed God's eternal life to enter Adam. The Ruach imparts the active power of God's creative image and the guiding light of His divine, redemptive nature into man. Whenever God's light comes upon or arises within us, our eyes are illumined to see past the natural and into the divine supernatural. Because we are now moving in the Spirit, we are able to see and be spiritual. The living God, the inspirational ingenious Ruach breath of Elohim, moves upon individuals and enables them to speak, produce and act on behalf of God.

> *To experience a positive, life-changing event, we must rouse our imaginations to know the dimensions of our true selves.*

Thanks be unto God who has redeemed my life from going down to the pit of destruction, that my spirit may be enlightened and my life shall see the light of the living (Job 33:28, 30). When the Lord lifts up the light of His favorable countenance upon us, He illuminates both the secrets of our hearts and our sinfulness, so that we may repent and only imagine good things. *That good thing which was committed to you, keep by the Holy Spirit who dwells in us* (2 Timothy 1:14).

> *The Lord is the light of my salvation, so I have no reason to dread the darkness. Even the darkness hides nothing from You, but the night shines as the day; the darkness and the light are both alike to You. In His light we see light. The light of God's truth leads us until it brings us to the holy hill and to His dwelling places* (Psalm 43:3).

Jesus is the light of the world. Therefore, let us walk in the light of the Lord. He covers Himself with a garment of light. Those who follow Jesus do not have to walk in darkness; they wear the shining garment of eternal light. God is the Father of Lights. *For it is the God who commanded light to shine out of darkness, who has shone in our hearts to give the light of the knowledge of the glory of God in the face of Jesus Christ* (2 Corinthians 4:6).

The entrance and unfolding of God's Word give light unto our path and understanding, spiritual discernment and the comprehension of truth to the simple. The Holy Spirit shines light upon the path of those who love Jesus.

God forms the light and creates darkness, He makes a nation be at peace and He creates physical evil or calamity; He is the Lord, Who does all these things (Isaiah 45:7).

Grace and favor are the building blocks that come to us before the glory of God is released in our lives. Jesus is the only way to God's love, deliverance, healing and salvation. His light is sown for the uncompromising righteous and is strewn along their pathway. The irrepressible joy of the Lord falls upon the upright in heart when they are conscious of God's grace, favor, joy and protection.

Some question why they have not seen the favor of God released or manifested in their life as they have requested or in the way they have expected. We must bear in mind that God does not give a person favor or fame in order for them to receive the accolades of man. Platforms of influence are built and given to lift God's names out of the shadows into a glorious light

> *We rule and take dominion through the knowledge of Christ, who called us to speak to both the spiritual world of beings and the tangible, physical things in the earthly realms as God's glory and His great virtues direct us.*

of His manifested presence. Those who willingly lose their life in order to serve God's purposes on earth, indeed, receive untold promises and glorious rewards.

> *Jesus called the crowd of people to join His disciples who were already standing around Him: "If any of you intend to follow Me, you must let Me lead. You will not be able to run from suffering; but I will show you how to embrace, endure and overcome it. Self-help is not the answer but self-sacrifice is My way to save your true self. What good would come to you if you got everything you wanted yet lost your true soul's identity that is found only in Me? If you are embarrassed of Me in front of*

your fickle, unfocused friends, know that you will be an even greater embarrassment to the Son of Man when He arrives in all the splendor of God His Father, with an army of holy angels and you have not been transformed into His image or likeness" (Mark 8:34–38).

God will become our everlasting light when we end the days of our mourning.

So, we are to arise from the depression and prostration in which circumstances have kept us—to rise to a new life! Shine, be radiant with the glory of the Lord, for our light has come, and the glory of the Lord has risen upon us. And nations shall come to our light and kings to the brightness of our rising (Isaiah 60:1–3).

When we pray each new morning, God brings His justice to light. When we know what God is saying and doing, others certainly take notice. Kings, presidents and national leaders from all around the world will seek us out and say, *I have heard of you, that the Spirit of the holy God is in you and that light and understanding and superior wisdom are found in you* (Daniel 5:14).

Just as Daniel and Joseph of old rose to the top of their fields and were called before the Pharaohs of their time to interpret dreams, visions and to explain confusing enigmas, we, as Spirit-filled forerunners, will also be called to hear God's voice on the behalf of presidents and to give counsel to world leaders. *By Me, kings reign and rulers decree justice* (Proverbs 8:15).

> *We are a speaking spirit that has been given spiritual authority to imagine, see, say, pray, prophesy, decree, declare and dream about what God is doing.*

Prophets, like Solomon, who are able to hear the strategic voice of God, interpret His ways and see how to follow God's wise counsel, will draw a prestigious audience from the highest walks of life. Seers will entertain the privileged influencers like the Queen of Sheba who visited King Solomon with her select entourage of front-runner people.

Dr. Barbie L. Breathitt

As Believers, we are called to shine brightly as a beacon for Christ. *Let your light so shine before men that they may see your moral excellence and your praiseworthy, noble, and good deeds and recognize and honor and praise and glorify your Father who is in heaven* (Matthew 5:16). By allowing God's guiding light to luminously blaze from within us, we draw those in darkness unto Christ. Like the moth that lives in darkness is drawn to light, so those in darkness will be drawn to the fiery light of His shining until they are consumed and transformed into His likeness.

The revelatory light of God shining in and through the mature Believer will shatter the darkness with God's answers of hope and freedom. Each person who is born again is a shining light. As each light joins the kingdom of light, a city of heavenly lights will arise to pierce the darkness.

A bright city that shines with the light of God cannot be hidden. We are called to let our light so shine before men that they may see our moral excellence, our praiseworthy, noble and good deeds and recognize, honor and praise the Father of Glory.

> *The eye is the lamp of the body. So, if our eye is sound, our entire body will be full of God's eternal light. But if our eye is unsound, our whole body will be full of darkness. If then the very light in our conscience is darkened, how dense is that darkness* (Matthew 6:22–23).

God's illuminating light within us—His presence—allows us to enter into rest. It is at rest that our self-striving ceases and God, with all His power, wisdom and purposes, thrives within and through us.

CHAPTER ELEVEN

Entering Into Rest

God created by using the light of His words, wisdom, truth and the energetic, faith-focused power of His consciousness. At the same time God created, He also calculated, formed and retained all the answers to every question that would ever be asked. The Holy Spirit placed in reserve the wise responses to any prayer that would ever be prayed. God, the One who knows the end from the beginning, created man and the whole universe in just six days.

Man's beginning commenced as God's work concluded. *God blessed them (for Eve was within Adam), and God spoke to them, "Be fruitful and multiply (replenish), fill the earth and subdue it and have dominion over the entire world"* (Genesis 1:28). God ended the creative work of all that He had made on the sixth day. I will explain more on the significance of the number six later in the next chapter.

On the seventh day, God's work was done, and He rested. Creation is complete! *Thus, the heavens and the earth were completed, and all the host of them* (Genesis 2:1). God blessed and sanctified the seventh day as a day of rest.

> *And on the seventh day, the canvas of the cosmos was completed, so God paused from His labor of love. He ended His work, which He had done. God blessed the seventh day and made it a special time of pause and restoration. He rested on the seventh*

> *day in a sacred Sabbath zone from all the creative work which*
> *He had done* (Genesis 2:2–3; see Isaiah 42:5; 45:18).

God modeled a day of rest for Adam. God did this so that we, like Adam, would know how to obtain the words of promise that are attached to the things God had spoken into existence. The first thing Adam learned was how to relate to God from a place of rest. He knew what it was to enter into rest. Adam dwelt there, settled in a state of peaceful support and made his abode with and in God. Adam emerged from his resting place in order to relate to God from a space of inhabited rest. Adam became enlightened with God consciousness from a position of occupied rest. Through a place of tranquil peace and rest, Adam discovered the unlimited dimensions of the God who created him. Adam learned to trust in all of God's divine abilities as he dwelt in the rest of God's presence.

> *We are created in God's image with a mouth to speak to, pray about, decree, declare and prophesy about that which we are conscious of being.*

The first man walked and talked with God; their golden glory clouds collided and intermingled as one in the restful times of the cool, still evenings. There was no way to distinguish where God's glory cloud ended and Adam's began, for they were one in the Spirit of God consciousness. *It is the Spirit of God that made me which has stirred me up, and the Ruach breath of the Almighty that created me gives me life which inspires me* (Job 33:4).

The Eternal God conversed with man. God shared His imaginative thoughts with Adam. God communicated with Adam about every sort of animal, insect, fish and bird He designed and sculpted. Then God summoned and brought a procession of the Garden creatures before Adam. The Almighty Creator of the universe gave Adam (His highest creation) the authority to correctly perceive the internal nature and instinct of each creature and to name them. The prophet Isaiah wrote, *"You will keep him in perfect peace, whose mind* ('yester' means the creative, right side of the imagination's ability to conceptualize, conceive, do the needed work to frame our world) *is stayed on You, because he trusts in You* (Isaiah 25:3).

Out of Adam's spiritual ability to rest in God, the creative intuitions and his peace-filled insights came. The left side of our mind is for gathering and correlating information, as it brings things into a logical order. The right side is the imaginative, creative side of the brain that hears the Word of God, sees and understands the images God projects by His Spirit. God's overshadowing presence graced Adam's immagination with the skilled ability to determine each animal's respective nature, personality, disposition and makeup as he saw fit.

Based on God's established model for Adam, it is important for Believers to learn how to enter into God's rest in order to accomplish and establish prophesy, answered prayer, healing or anything else. God's divine power has been given to us, so that we can obtain All Things that pertain to experiencing life and godliness. We acquire the promises of God

> As long as man remains and operates in the carnal, natural level of his existence, the serpent has access to bite or devour him.

through patiently resting in His presence. As we, like Adam, learn how to enter in and remain at rest in the Spirit, we will move in a full measure of God's grace and peace. Without entering into rest, we will never obtain the promises of God. We must take on the future image of the spoken words decreed over us in order to rest in and manifest the creative dimension of the prophetic. If we do not agree with and rest in who God says we are, we will never become who we are destined to be.

As Believers, we are called to reflect God's true, immense, loving nature. We rule and take dominion through the knowledge of Christ, who called us to speak to both the spiritual world of beings and the tangible, physical things in the earthly realms as God's glory and His great virtues direct us. We have been given exceedingly abundant, numerous, valuable and precious promises that empower us to speak in the authority of God. *The spiritual, life-giving words we speak endow us to become partakers of God's divine nature* (2 Peter 1:2–4).

We procure a creative spiritual rest when we attain to a state of being and have focused our imagination on manifesting the presence of that promise for six consecutive days. However, these six days are not the designated twenty-four-hour days of the week we are accustomed to. These six days are an undetermined, consecutive, yet varied, focused and creative time period that causes us to rest in a new future realm of manifested authority. It may be a short, momentary time period, for some, perhaps just days, or, depending on the individual's lack of faith and discipline, it could span over years. When the end result, that God has purposed, is believed and sustained as our new reality, we emerge as a new being in a different, strengthened identity that is well able to exhibit and maintain our intended goals.

If we are successful in demonstrating the end result of what we have imagined, seen, dreamed, heard or spoken, a new state of existence is born in us. The divine promise is apprehended and our desired new state is congealed and takes form. If we are able to consistently keep and preserve that estate, it will be resurrected, released and birthed in us. Our imagination will arouse our new identity to catch the imaginative, Ruach, creative wind of the Spirit and come forth from its eternal resting place. And whatever we have believed, seen, imagined, and focused upon will manifest on the seventh day, so we can rest in it.

> *Changes begin to take place when we learn to watch over our dreams, discipline our imagination and thought life and control the inner conversations we hold with ourselves or about others.*

As we continue to rest in retaining that newly formed identity, having already obtained the promise, we move into a higher state of being. We take up residence in that spiritual mansion that has always been prepared for us by Christ. It has been waiting for us to come to where He is in the Father's house. *And when* (if) *I go and make ready a place for you, I will come back again and will take you to Myself, that where I am you may be also. And to the place where I am going, you know the way* (John 14:3–4, 6).

Jesus went before us into the Spirit to show our imagination the way of spiritual knowledge, eternal life and truth. The Spirit of Christ within us gives us the ability to navigate the spiritual realms to find Jesus waiting for us in one of the many mansions in His Father's house.

Resting in God's truth empowers everything we touch or endeavor to do to increase, multiply and prosper until it turns into a cloud of golden glory that causes Christ's reality to permeate everything that pertains to us. To experience a positive, life-changing event, we must rouse our imaginations to know the dimensions of our true selves.

Personal Reflection Moment

To rouse your imagination to know your true self, you must define who you are presently by examining yourself and your circumstances. Below are some poignant questions you may want to consider:

1. What are my strengths and weaknesses?

2. What do I believe?

3. What opportunities are present?

4. What obstacles need to be removed?

5. What type of root troubles need to be identified and overcome?

6. What measure of faith and power do I currently possess?

7. What do I need to let go of, grow in and alter in order to make room for more faith and truth?

When an adequate evaluation of our present state is completed and dually noted, we must make decisions regarding what needs to be enhanced or changed. We strive to transform in order to agree with becoming the grand person who God has always desired for us to be. With the objective of transmuting into who God affirms we are, we set goals and keep abreast of checkmarks to bring about that transformation. It is wise to continue checking ourselves in order to maintain the veracity of our states of being. We do this by reviewing and evaluating our objectives and current status.

Personal Reflection Moment

1. What are my current aims or goals in life?

2. Are they easily obtainable or realistically achievable?

3. Am I incorporating the power of my imagination and dreams in the process?

4. Am I stsaying focused on obtaining my goals? Am I staying on track or wandering aimlessly?

Entering into rest is to enter into the harmony of God's presence. In His presence, all is in order and at peace—where God has a plan for His beloveds to join Him in experiencing His rest. We enter into rest when we have come into one accordpeace with an idea, when we have accepted that idea as a truth. We have seen it. We have entered into faith and believe it to be real. In doing so, we are now able to actualize it; so it becomes part of us. We rest in God's truthit. His peaceIt comes to live and reside in us. Christ's creative Spirit rests in us. The promises of God are activated or actualized through a spirit of rest.

CHAPTER TWELVE

Gestation and Increase

God assigned the number six to man—His greatest design. The number six depicts the weakness of man and indicates man's incompleteness through his toiling and wrestling with both the carnal and the spiritual natures in the physical world. As long as man remains and operates in the carnal, natural level of his existence, the serpent has access to bite or devour him. With the imagination awakened, we can operate in the spiritual level.

We are created in God's image with a mouth to speak to, pray about, decree, declare and prophesy about that which we are conscious of being. God has given man six days (an undetermined amount of earthly time) in order to speak the world we desire into existence and to execute all of our creative work.

Because man is the only being or existing thing in which God dwells, I believe the number six is more important than any other symbolism. Let's take a look at several biblical examples that highlight and illustrate the significance of the six days of creating and executing.

There were six vessels of water at the wedding feast of Cana. This is where Jesus performed His first creative miracle. When Jesus stood before six containers full of plain water (The human body is comprised of 70 percent water; these six pots represent six ordinary men.), He (Creator of the earth, Author of perfect love) was able to transform one molecular substance, form or structure (ordinary man) into the best of wine (Holy Spirit-filled joy in people) the steward (expert connoisseur) had ever tasted (see John 2:6-11).

It can take six days of focused prayer to create or frame a new door of entry with the spoken Word of God.

> *By faith we understand that the worlds during the successive ages were framed, fashioned, put in order and equipped for their intended purpose, by the word of God, so that what we see was not made out of things which are visible* (Hebrews 11:3).

The words we speak form a passageway that opens to establish a new attitude, exhibit broader goals or to adopt a different aspect of God's expanded Kingdom (see Exodus 20:9).

The Creator of the universe swept into being the spangled heavens (and all its host) and the earth in six days. *For the Eternal made the heavens above, the earth below, the seas, and all the creatures in them in six days. Then, on the seventh day, He rested. That is why God blessed the Sabbath Day and made it sacred* (Exodus 20:11).

While Israel wandered in the desert, the Spirit of God commanded them, *You are to gather manna* (the miraculous food of heavenly revelation) *for your provisions for six days, but on the seventh day* (the Sabbath of rest), *none of the manna from heaven will be on the ground* (Exodus 16:26).

> *During a time of national drought, the prophet Elijah went up to the top of Carmel; and he bowed himself down upon the earth and put his face between his knees in a birthing position. And said to his servant, "Go up now, look* (use your imagination and spiritual sense of sight) *toward the sea." And he went up six times and looked and said, "There is nothing." Elijah said, "Go again seven times." And at the seventh time, the servant said, "I see a* (glory) *cloud as small as a man's hand* (that contains five fingers; 'five-fold' ministry) *is arising out of the sea." And Elijah said, "Go up, and say what you see to Ahab. Tell Ahab to take action and do the Word of the Lord.*

Dr. Barbie L. Breathitt

Hitch your chariot and go down, lest the rain stop you" (1 Kings 18:42–44).

As Believers, we are empowered to see what God is doing. We are a speaking spirit that has been given spiritual authority to imagine, see, say, pray, prophesy, decree, declare and dream about what God is doing. We are to become doers of the Word. By assuming the identity of God, we take up the creative actions we see Him doing. Doers of the Word become achievers who recognize the challenges of life, gladly take them on and productively take action. Observing what the Father is doing in heaven sanctions us to mimic His actions here on earth by doing what God has said and demonstrated.

Another example in Scripture of the number six manifesting increase is when the patriarch Moses made his way up the mountain.

> *There he was engulfed in a thick cloud that blanketed the mountain; Eternal's glory had settled upon it. The dark, thick cloud remained at rest there on the mountaintop for six days. When the seventh day arrived, the Eternal God spoke to Moses from the glory cloud* (Exodus 24:15–16).

When we walk and talk with God in the cloud of glory (like Adam did in the Garden and Moses on the mountain top), we enter into a position of intimate, abiding rest; we commune with the overshadowing, impregnating and powerful presence of God. *The Sabbath exists as a sign forever of the covenant between God and the people of Israel for He made heaven and earth in six days, but then on the seventh day He stopped His work and was refreshed* (Exodus 31:17). Seven represents the seven days of creation, completeness, wholeness, fullness and spiritual perfection before Passover to enter into rest.

> *We are to work for six days* (Focus on imagining, speaking, praying and prophesying what we see. We then declare and decree the Word of God, so that the light of God can establish that thing. Focus your faith on this process of creating in order to manifest a new idea, miracle or concept of the Kingdom of God.), *but when the seventh day of fullness arrives, we are to observe* (see what our imagination has cre-

ated) *the Sabbath and rest in its completion. Even when it is the time to plow* (break up the fallow ground) *and harvest* (reap or complete what we have sown or thought in order to obtain the promised reward), *we must still enter in and remain at rest on the seventh day* (Exodus 34:21).

When God wanted the walls of Jericho to fall down, He had Israel unite as one spiritual, influential unit and march around the massive walls for six consecutive days. *Every day for the next six days, you will march once around the city walls with all your fighting force* (Joshua 6:3). Israel's faith continued as an integrated, focused force that persistently moved in one direction.

God also had Joshua command the people to hold their voice until a predetermined time had arrived. He understood the creative power of words that are aligned and in agreement for a specific purpose. *You shall not shout or let your voice be heard, nor shall any word proceed out of your mouth until the day I tell you to shout! Then you shall shout in one accord* (Joshua 6:10).

The nation of Israel's six days of marching in a consistent, silent movement was followed on by an earth-shattering sound of a culminating trumpet blast and a long, loud unified shout of victory on the seventh day. Seven priests with seven trumpets marched around Jericho seven times. When their final march ended, Joshua instructed the whole nation of people, "Shout! For the Lord has given you the city!" The seven priests blew a great, harmonious trumpet blast combined with Israel's great shout of confidence in their God. Israel released a new sound that caused the walled obstacle to crumble and fall. Israel moved over and past the massive, fallen walls into their promise and took possession of their great rewards (see Hebrews 11:30). Remember, seven is God's number of fullness (where we develop into wholeness, culminate into the final completion of spiritual perfection).

The following final two Scripture excerpts furthermore demonstrate the significance of a specific time lapse of six days (the time of imagining creation) that occurs to position us at the right place at the right time:

> *Six days after, Jesus said, "Truly some of you who are here now will not experience death before you see the Kingdom of God coming in glory and power." Jesus led Peter, James, and John*

up to a high mountaintop. There, Jesus was transformed, from the inside out, into His glorious image right before their eyes. Jesus' clothes shimmered and glistened white. Elijah and Moses came into view and engaged in deep conversation with Jesus. Suddenly, a radiant, light-filled cloud engulfed all of them (just like the all-encompassing glory cloud covered Adam as he walked with God in the Garden). *The Father's voice spoke from deep within, "This is My Son, marked by My love. Listen to Him."* (Mark 9:2–7; Matthew 17:1–6).

When Believers become conscious of the omnipotent, omniscient, omnipresent Christ who dwells within, they will be transfigured and lifted up into His image and likeness. Christ learned how to unlock and release the resurrection power resident within His body. Can you imagine the glory that was released on the mountain of transfiguration as the disciples witnessed his glorious ascension into heaven (see Luke 24:50)?

Jesus learned how to master the assembly and the disassembly of every cell of his body. Jesus could transfigure into a radiant, sun-like cloud of glory, commune with the great cloud of witnesses, walk on water, raise the dead and escape death by walking invisibly through an angry, rock-fisted mob that attempted to throw him off a cliff.

Science has proven the devastating, destructive power that is held in one solitary atom. When that power is used by natural forces and is released in war, it can destroy hundreds of miles in any massive, geographic area. Now imagine the dunamis power that is resident in every cell of the Spirit-filled Believer. We can learn to harness that same Holy Spirit power just as Christ did. Mastering and channeling God's divine light that is resident within our cells and deep within our bone marrow will release the creative realm of miracles to manifest through the Believer.

Six days before the Passover feast (the time when we die to the old and leave one dimension or season of life behind in order to be resurrected into a new, better life in a higher, freer realm of existence), *Jesus journeyed to the village of Bethany, to the home of Lazarus who Jesus had recently raised from the dead when it was absolutely impossible because Lazarus' spirit had left his body. The entombed, shrouded body of Lazarus stunk, because he had been dead for four days* (John

12:1).

Jesus always demonstrated a single-minded, heavenly perspective that was focused on His Father. Jesus remained concentrated on God's will in order to obtain His true happiness and success. In order for us to obtain success, the kingdom of heaven must first be made manifest on earth within our individual lives. Thenceforward, God's Kingdom must flow into every aspect of society—into our families, businesses, schools, communities, government, ministries and churches.

The dominion of the Kingdom shall be given to the Believers of the Most High God; for His Kingdom is an everlasting kingdom. The saints of God are to be envied for their spiritual prosperity because they are blessed and highly favored. The children of God who are persecuted for righteousness sake will inherit the Kingdom of God. But those who do not take up their cross to daily follow Jesus and conform to His example of righteous living are not worthy of salvation. If anyone desires to be Christ's disciple, that person must cleave steadfastly to Christ and His ways and deny himself by losing sight of his own selfish interests.

Your righteous testimonies are everlasting, and Your decrees are binding to eternity; give me understanding, and I shall live. Give me discernment and comprehension, and I shall not die (Psalm 119:144).

I often find myself asking God, "What is man that You are mindful of him? And the son of man that You visit him?"

We know eternity resides within the heart of man; God placed a guiding portion of Himself deep within the imaginative core of our being. At the moment of microscopic conception, when the sperm and egg meet, God places a small portion of His eternal light of life within each and every person. *God has made everything beautiful in its time. Also, He has put eternity in their hearts, except that no one can find out the work that God does from beginning to end* (Ecclesiastes 3:11).

God dwells in an eternally higher realm of existence than man. The God of eternity is always dwelling within the Believer, calling him or her upward into His Father's house to be renewed into His image and his or her consciousness to be restored into His likeness. God dwells within the humble, contrite heart of His children.

For thus says the High and Lofty One who inhabits eternity, whose name is Holy: *I dwell in the high and holy place, with him who has a contrite and humble spirit, to revive the spirit of the humble, and to revive the (imaginative) heart of the contrite ones* (Isaiah 57:15).

Beyond Eternity

Only in the realm of God's timing
Would a visionary glimpse be granted,
Of that which exists in the experience
Beyond the imaginations of this earthly realm.
Eternity's conceptual picture leaves us wanting,
In our stretch to even paint a mental picture,
Much less anything that would have to carry us
Into realms of the fourth dimension beyond, ad infinitum.

Keat Wade 02/05/18 (20 Sh'vat 5778)

Believers are designed to live in, move with and sustain their being in God. When the cloud of glory hovers or the pillar of fire (illuminated thought) advances in the night, we are to pick up our tent (our body, Temple of God) and move with the presence of God. We must be ever alert to the changes that need to occur for this to be possible.

Personal Reflection Moment

Continually observe your thoughts and behaviors; they will predict your measure of success by determining your state of being. The answers to the following questions will serve as a barometer if you are truly resting in His truth.

1. Do you impulsively react, energetically recreate or respond in a proactive manner?

2. How do you respond under pressure? Do you often recoil?

3. Do you strike out at others in anger?

4. Do you feel rejection or disappointment in response to the outcomes of various events or relations with others?

Changes begin to take place when we learn to watch over our dreams, discipline our imagination and thought life and control the inner conversations we hold with ourself or about others. All of these factors motivate our outer responses. By prayerfully altering or eliminating the negative manners in which we answer the questions, challenges and opportunities, we are able to repent and ascend up another rung of Jacob's heavenly ladder. When we choose to climb another rung of the ladder, our imagination will arise, mount up with wings and go before us to prepare the way.

Let's Pray

Dear Jesus, You are the Creator of heaven and earth. You alone are the Almighty, Eternal God. We come before Your throne of grace to worship You in spirit and in truth. We are conscious that All Things came into being and exist in and through You. You are the only door of access to Father God.

We submit ourselves to You, Your divine will and Your perfect plans and destinies for our lives. We boldly ask that You recreate us fresh and anew in Your divine image and likeness. Enfold us into Christ as entirely new creations. Vanish all that pertains to the old order, and make everything fresh and new. Open the eyes of our hearts to be enlightened to see Your beauty and know the hope to which You have called us. Make us to be the riches of Your glorious inheritance as Your holy people.

Help us to grow in love, exercising the spiritual fruits and functioning in all of the gifts of the Spirit. Tune our ears to hear the wisdom that rings forth from Your voice. Because we believe, may the Father give us the Spirit of Wisdom and Revelation so that we may know Him better as His incomparable great power is exercised on our behalf. Strengthen our bodies to serve Your purposes here on this earth. Empower us by the Spirit of Your Might, and wrap the light of Your glory around us so that we are able to bring the demonstration of God's Kingdom forth on earth as it is in heaven. Anoint us with the ability to preach the good news of the gospel to the poor. Empower us to bind up the wounds of the brokenhearted and dispel darkness in order to set captives free.

We embrace the full delivering power of salvation so that our thoughts are protected from lies. We take up the sharp, spiritual Word of God. Having taken on His divine nature, we speak it forth in the name, characters and attributes of God. Teach us to pray passionately in the Spirit and with our understanding at all times. Amen.

Author's Note

In Volume II of the *IMAGINE* series, we will continue to explore the astounding workings of the sanctified imagination. We will discover and unwrap our new identity in Christ and advancement in the glory realm to fulfill our destinies in the calling of being and manifesting as the Sons of God.

About the Author

DR. BARBIE L. BREATHITT

DR. BARBIE BREATHITT is a certified prophetic life coach (Ask-Barbie.com), published best-selling author, dedicated educator and experienced revelatory teacher of the divine, supernatural manifestations of God, whose greatest desire is to see other reach, fullfill and enjoy their destiny in God. She is recognized around the world as a leading master dream analyst (DreamsDecoder.com) and healing evangelist with deliverance, signs, wonders and creative miracles following. Barbie's prophetic seer gifting and deep spiritual insights have helped and equipped thousands of people, including business, media and government leaders, and ministries in over 40 nations understand God's mystical ways.

Dr. Barbie Breathitt teaches individuals, trains corporate professionals and business teams, government leaders and churches how to recognize, respond to and release the activity of God with unique strategies. Her sincere pursuit of God's Kingdom and His eternal truth make Barbie's Texas-based Breath of the Spirit Ministries, Inc. a predominant worldwide foundation.

An experienced teacher, published author, prophetic voice, dream analyst and healing evangelist, she has released God's love, presence and breath in prisons, hospitals, streets, Europe, third-world nations, television, radio and the internet. Her deepest desire is to see people fulfill their unique destiny here on earth. Barbie's training, resources and personal ministry help others to interpret and apply the direction God gives them through encounters, dreams and visions.

Barbie Breathitt personally learned and now passionately teaches God's Love, Presence and Breath. Her astute prophetic voice and accurate dream analyses have blessed those in prisons, hospitals, Europe and third-world nations, enabling many hungry people to grow. Barbie has abandoned herself to the Holy Spirit with miracles, signs and wonders following. Many individuals have been miraculously healed in her meetings while others have experienced the Presence of the Spirit as never before. Her infectious humor promotes unity with those inside and outside the church walls.

An ordained healing evangelist, Barbie has ministered for over thirty-five years around the world. Barbie established and conducted three prophetic training centers. Barbie now lives in Texas and opened Breath of the Spirit Center of Training in 2004. Breath of the Spirit offers a variety of courses on Healing, Revelatory Gifts, Dream Interpretation and Evangelistic Outreaches.

SPEAKING ENGAGEMENTS

Traveling around the world to share wisdom and insights regarding sound, biblical dream interpretation, Barbie is available for conferences, teaching and hands-on training. Please contact Barbie's ministry at Breath of the Spirit Ministries, Inc. through email (info@DreamsDecoder.com), the website (DreamsDecoder.com) or by phone at (972) 253-6653 for more information.

The *IMAGINE* Series

Volume I will help you understand and fully comprehend that the Spirit of Christ dwells mightily within your sanctified imagination. Discover how to supplant the carnal mindset that has limited God and the displaying of His grandeur in your life. By resting in and experiencing the presence and glory of God, you will be empowered to receive and harness His truth, divine wisdom, revelation and supernatural faith to confidently realize, embrace and achieve your unique purpose and grand destiny in this new era!

God has given you a riveting new identity in this new era! Volume II inspires and imparts how to further unlock and mature your imagination to fulfill God's purposes for your life. Discover what it is and how to shed your worldly, carnal self—how to transition into your higher IAM state of being in Christ. Advance beyond the limitations of the third dimension, and gain supernatural knowledge of the mysterious workings of the unrestrictive, four-dimensional realm of the Spirit.

The marvelous design and divine workings of the inspired imagination is further unveiled in this third volume. You will gain applicable spiritual understanding of how to access, unlock and interpret the meanings of visions and dreams that God skillfully fashions within your imagination. You will discover how to access your God-given authority. You will unite with the Fire of God to believe, see and prophesy in the NOW realm of God's faith. Through a broadened understanding of God's Word and clear spiritual insights into the profound power of imaginative prayer, you will be able to access the answers to your prayers that have been waiting on you to discover from the Genesis of creation. *IMAGINE* Volume III will equip and fully transition you into your new and glory-purposed identity in Christ. Your faith in God will explode into the supernatural faith of God!

In this instructive and illuminating volume, you will gain divine knowledge about the healing power of the subconscious, God's imaginative power and creative miracles. Volume IV will challenge what you believe, see and reason as truth and will help you identify the hindrances to having your prayers answered. God is restoring His people as One New Man! By using your sanctified imagination, you will discover how to come into agreement with God in order to effectively release your prophetic voice in this new era. You will obtain valuable instruction on how to increase, advance and prosper for God's kingdom purposes.

This fifth volume of the *IMAGINE* series brings the concepts learned in previous volumes full circle. Now that you have believed, beheld and obtained your new identity, you will discover the keys to successfully maintain that identity. You will encounter God's creative power, divine desire, godly disciplines of the imagination and lasting growth. The time to advance is NOW! Volume V delivers sound biblical teachings of how to use your creative imagination to release and prophesy into your God-ordained destiny and the destinies of nations. You will acquire the necessary knowledge and wisdom to effectively operate, persevere and prosper as a true Son of God and as One New Man.

DECODEMYDREAM.COM

ONLINE DREAM JOURNAL

Barbie Breathitt is excited that so many people in God's Kingdom are exploring the understanding of dreams. Barbie's 30 years of study and experience in biblically-based, spirit-led dream interpretation are available in an online learning experience.

DreamsDecoder.com and DecodeMyDream.com are our interactive web sites, impacting dreamers all over the world. We believe it is vitally important to record God-given dreams and to search out the messages they contain. The site provides a free online dream journal, dream evaluations, dream mapping, prophetic analysis and comprehensive dream certification training.

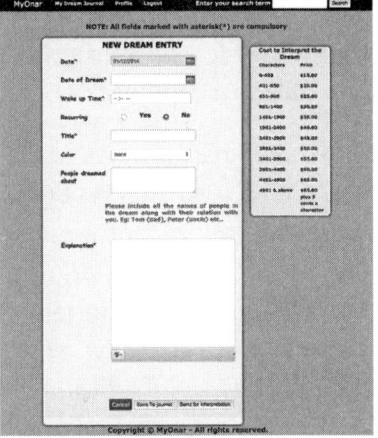

Sign up for your free online dream journal at DreamsDecoder.com. From the dream journal, you can easily submit your dreams for analysis by Barbie and our highly skilled dream analysts.

For additional resources by Dr. Barbie L. Breathitt, please visit
DreamsDecoder.com
Breath of the Spirit Ministries, Inc.
PO Box 1356 | Lake Dallas, TX 75065
(972) 253-6653

BOOKS

Dream Encounters–Seeing Your Destiny from God's Perspective is the "Rosetta Stone" to interpreting the illusive vapors of dreams. Uniquely inspired, and written to convince the greatest skeptics, and educate the most ardent believer, "Dream Encounters" will bring God's perspective, and understanding to the symbolic, visual, love letters, in the mysterious world of dreams. Take a journey into the sub–conscious night parables of the soul, to learn how dream truths impact your world; give direction, purpose, and destiny.  Gain valuable keys to success by unlocking the mysteries of your dreams. Available as a paperback book, digital book or audio book.

Gateway to the Seer Realm: Look Again to See Beyond the Natural is written by Dr. Barbie Breathitt a gifted Seer who has years of personal experience interpreting dreams and ministering in the prophetic realm. You will gain valuable insights into understanding the ways of God and the divine supernatural realms of vision, dreams, angels, healing and destiny. Open new dimensions of revelation knowledge to learn how to access the Seer realm through intimate daily communication with God.

Dream Seer: Searching for the Face of the Invisible is written by Dr. Barbie L. Breathitt to help the reader understand the Seer Realms of angels, divine visions, the voice and presence of the Lord and dimensions where the ethereal vapors of our dreams will become substantial presences when we believe that anything is possible with God. God is the giver of dreams. Jesus is also the Redeemer. So, like a knight in shining armor, He comes to restore the dreams we have allowed to fall by the wayside. The Holy Spirit inspires us to recall the images He sent long ago. God has mapped out our future. He brings the events of the world to bear on our individual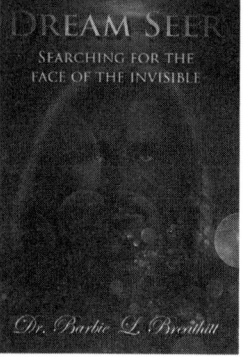

circumstances as He wills. When the events of our lives coincide with the correct timing of His plans, the next phase of our destiny ensues. The Holy Spirit knows the perfect time to bring the dreams and plans He has formulated to enable our purpose to come to pass.

There is only one right interpretation, God's. Every thing else is only shades of gray. Dream Interpreter will give you skill to correctly decipher the symbolism of your dreams. *Dream Interpreter* decodes symbols, types and shadows of images from a heavenly perspective in order to reveal the hidden mysteries that are contained within. Dream Interpreter will help the reader translate spiritual perceptions and happenings to accurately discern the events of the night. The gifted dream interpreter can decipher, convert and transform a concealed secret and then develop a blueprint for prosperity. You can learn to understand the evolution of vivid visions and dreams, the graphic picture language of nightmares and night terrors that come to visit and present truth about one's life. As a wise counsellor or life coach, dream interpreters fashion destiny bubbling up from the depths of the person's soul-potential to successfully guide the dreamer.

Acquiring a working knowledge of dream symbolism will enhance your ability to decipher the profound meanings of each symbol and then unlock the interpretation of every one of your dreams. Knowledge is power so learn to understand the mysteries that are hidden in your dreams. Their divine secrets will release your concealed potential so that you can design the destiny you have always longed for. Access the revelation knowledge stored in the pages of *A to Z Dream Symbology Dictionary*. Glean from ten thousand keywords and symbolic meanings that will inspire you to delve deeper into understanding why a certain animal, object, person, place, vehicle, article of clothing, tool, home, food, flower, weather pattern, action, emotion, color, or number appeared in your subconscious dream.

In her book, *Angels in God's Kingdom*, Dr. Barbie L. Breathitt propels readers beyond a natural understanding of the world around them to perceive and navigate the divine supernatural realms of the invisible world of angels. This one-of-a-kind comprehensive Biblical resource is full of progressive revelation and inspired spiritual truths. Dr. Barbie L. Breathitt covers fascinating topics detailing the origin, existence, and abode of angelic beings, their names, ministry functions, duties, and little known facts about the classifications of angels. She explores the nature

of angels, the bold power of active faith and how the anointings of angels, seraphim, cherubim, heavenly creatures and host connect and guide us to and through the spirit world. Barbie shares her real life angelic encounters and the knowledge she has received through her diverse visitations, as well as her traumatic experience with the spirit of death. Discover the mystery of how recognizing the presence of powerful angels can redeem time when they are invited to step out of eternity to assist us in miracles, healing and deliverance. Learn how to prosper as the angels in God's Kingdom collide with the lawless evil forces of darkness and destruction. Gain spiritual understanding of how God's holy, intelligent angels clash with Satan's demons and diabolical fallen angels in today's modern world. Discover how the giants from the days of Noah are currently affecting society. And how we can defeat them through the blood of Jesus.

When Will My Dreams Come True? This handy booklet provides valuable detailed descriptions on dreams, visions and spiritual encounters. The information shared in these pages will educate the dreamer on the biblical techniques of dream interpretation. Through the study and application of the Hebrew alphabet and numbers, you will develop an Issachar anointing to discern the days, times and seasons of your dreams coming to pass. This collection of data research, priceless dream interpretation nuggets, gradient echelons of revelation, and prophetic vocabulary and terminology assembled in these pages will instruct

dreamers on how to record and accurately interpret the meaning of their dreams, so they can pray, decree and declare them into being.

DREAM SYMBOL CARDS

These artistically designed dream symbol cards enable the dreamer to tap into the hidden meanings of the symbols that appear in many dreams and visions. These cards are also useful in helping the believer decipher the symbolic language that God uses to communicate through the revelatory realm of the Spirit. "God is speaking powerfully through dreams in this hour. So many believers are having significant dreams but do not always understand the significance of the symbols within them. Barbie Breathitt has done a marvellous job of preparing dream cards as a tremendous tool to help this process. They are very high quality and fully laminated for long-term use. I was impressed when I saw them." Patricia King XP Ministries (xpministries.com).

Acquire all of Barbie's artistically designed, laminated Dream Encounter Symbols Cards. They are available as single dream cards, in an excel spreadsheet or in spiral-bound collections.

Dream Encounters Symbols Volume I features the original 23 dream cards starter set with 1433 unique symbol definitions which makes an excellent gift for those who have a desire to learn the meanings of their dreams. The collection includes Animals, Apparel & Clothing, Body Parts, Color, Color and Music Healing, Creatures Great, Creatures Small, God's Dream Language, Going Places, Going More Places, Home Furnishings, Jewels, Musical Instruments, Numbers, People, Seers' Word of Knowledge Ministry Card, Spiritual, More Spiritual, Tools, U. S. State, Vehicles, and Weather and Natural Elements.

Dream Encounters Symbols Volume II has 18 different dream cards with 619 different symbol definitions. The collection includes Birds (4 dream symbol cards containing a myriad of positive and negative winged creatures), Bugs and Insects (3 cards), Money and Finance, Nutrition (5 cards outlining the meaning of different foods, sweets, meats and vegetables), Plants and Flowers (4 cards detail what different floral arrangements and bouquets represent. God is giving His Bride flowers in her dream. What is He saying to you?), and Varied contains a list of Frequent Dream Symbols.

Dream Encounters Symbols Volume III has an additional 29 spiral bound dream cards that combines 913 symbols complied in helpful categories for ease of study and use. The collection includes, Body Parts (an extensive compilation of 5 dream symbol cards), Building, Rooms & Structures (4 cards), People (12 individual cards listing careers, professions and callings), Spiritual & Military Weapons of War (4 dream symbol cards describing the spiritual weapons of prayer available to believers), and Vehicles (4 dream symbol cards boats, ships, trucks, cars, vans, airplanes, rockets and more).

Action Symbols Volume IV, has 13 artistically designed spiral bound dream symbol cards with 386 different movements such as flying, running, transporting, and translating actions.

Dream Sexology has 4 unique and informative dream symbol cards with 95 unique symbol definitions that explain the meanings of your intimate naked dream language.

Sports & Recreation Dream Symbols contains 13 dream symbol cards full of 321 different hobbies, sports, games and much more to help you take an active part in the game of life instead of sitting on the sidelines observing the excitement of others.

TEACHING SERIES

The Dream Encounter MP3 Downloads and Manual is designed to teach, train, activate, and impart the skills to interpret and understand how God communicates to us through dreams and visions of the night. Jesus continues to teach through night parables, in other words, inspired dreams. The Bible gives us three keys that will be used in

the end-time revival and outpouring of the Holy Spirit. The course topics include: Dreams, Visions, Transportations, Translations, Lucid Dreams, Colors, Numbers, Dream Symbols, Dream Interpretation, and Dream Teams and Outreaches.

The Revelatory Encounter MP3 Downloads and Manual is a prophetic course designed to teach, train, activate, and impart the ability to hear God's voice for yourself and others. This training helps you recognize and remove hindrances to hearing God's still, small voice. The course  topics include: Developing Godly Character and Integrity, Old and New Testament Prophets, False Prophets, Immature Prophets, God's Friends, Knowing God's Voice, Difference between the Gift of Prophecy and the Prophetic Office, Forms of Revelation, Four Categories of Prophecy, Spirit of Prophecy, Nine Gifts of the Holy Spirit, Interpretation, Application, The Seer, The Watchmen, Intercession, Prayer, Intimacy, Spiritual Authority, and Developing Prophetic Ministry Teams.

The Angelic Encounter MP3 downloads and Manual is a course that establishes a biblical foundation for the proof and ministry of angels. Topics include: What are Angels? Ministry of Angels; Types, Functions, and Characteristics of Angels; Satan and Fallen Angels; and Angels and the Death of the Saints. Barbie shares personal experiences of angelic visitations from her life.

The Healing Encounter MP3 Downloads and Manual is designed to teach, train, activate and impart the belief, skills and abilities to move in the healing ministry. Topics include: Introduction to Healing; Jesus, the Healer; Issues of the Heart; Four Aspects of Healing; The Faith Realm; Take Your Authority; You Get What You Expect; Miracles  Today; Hindrances to Miracles; Suffering in Regards to Healing; God's Voice of Healing; You Must See it to Be it!; Keep Your Healing; Healing Scriptures; Baptism with the Holy Spirit; and Walking in the Healing Ministry.

OTHER RESOURCES

The Hand Prayer Points Chart is a reference card that matches illnesses and diseases with prayer points on the hand. Great for intercessors who need clear direction for their prayers.

The Foot Prayer Points Chart is a reference card that matches the organs of the body, illnesses and diseases with prayer points on the foot. Great for intercessors who need clear direction for their prayers.

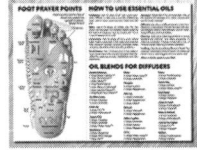

Healing Card is a reference card that matches illnesses and diseases with possible spiritual root causes. This Healing card is birthed from Barbie's ministry experiences and encounters of seasoned intercessors and those in healing ministries. Great for intercessors and individuals who need clear direction for their healing prayers.

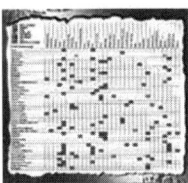

Waking Words of Ancient Wisdom Make it a practice to notice the time on the digital clock as you awaken from a spiritually significant dream. The numbers displayed on the digital clock are often keys to help understand the message God is giving you in your dreams. Note the time on your clock, then look up the corresponding chapter and verse in the Bible. Allow the Holy Spirit to quicken the intended "Waking Words of Ancient Wisdom" to your heart and apply them in your life. This is a wonderful way to daily explore the Bible while you seek the deeper meanings of the treasures God is revealing to you through your dreams. Visit BarbieBreathitt.com to obtain detailed directions for use.

Dream Encounter Anointing Oil: Anoint yourself every night with this fragrant dream enhancing oil and pray for the Holy Spirit to visit you in your sleep. You will experience a heightened level of dreams, visions and visitations from the Spirit of God.

My Thoughts

_____

_____

_____

_____

_____

_____

_____

_____

_____

_____

_____

_____

_____

_____

_____

_____

_____

_____

_____

_____